D0393224

SEEKING OUR BROTHERS

RESTORING COMPASSIONATE CHRISTIANITY TO THE CHURCH

BART PIERCE

© Copyright 2000—Bart Pierce

All rights reserved. This book is protected under the copyright laws of the United States of America. This book may not be copied or reprinted for commercial gain or profit. The use of short quotations or occasional page copying for personal or group study is permitted and encouraged. Permission will be granted upon request. Unless otherwise identified, Scripture quotations are from the New King James Version of the Bible. Scriptures marked KJV, NIV, and NRSV are taken from the King James Version, New International Version, and the New Revised Standard Version, respectively. Please note that Destiny Image's publishing style capitalizes certain pronouns in Scripture that refer to the Father, Son, and Holy Spirit, and may differ from some Bible publishers' styles.

Take note that the name satan and related names are not capitalized. We choose not to acknowledge him, even to the point of violating grammatical rules.

Fresh Bread

An Imprint of

Destiny Image® Publishers, Inc.
P.O. Box 310
Shippensburg, PA 17257-0310

ISBN 0-7684-2100-4

For Worldwide Distribution
Printed in the U.S.A.

This book and all other Destiny Image, Revival Press, MercyPlace, Fresh Bread, and Treasure House books are available at Christian bookstores and distributors worldwide.

For a U.S. bookstore nearest you, call **1-800-722-6774**.
For more information on foreign distributors, call **717-532-3040**.
Or reach us on the Internet: **http://www.reapernet.com**

Dedication

I dedicate this book to God, for His grace and favor in my life, and to my wife and best friend, Coralee. And I dedicate it to the countless number of people who are out there waiting for someone to reach out to them with a message of hope and healing.

Acknowledgments

A special thanks goes to Coralee, my wife of 30 years, who spent much time reading and typing, and loving and encouraging me every step of the way. She also shares the passion for reaching "the ones nobody wants." And to Rachel, Matt, and Josh, who have grown up with a dad whose passion has often taken him to those outside the home, and loved him for it. I also thank Brandi Ireland, who is always ready to respond and help. She has kept me on schedule and on time for all the hours of work that it takes to make a book like this a reality.

This book would never have happened without the help of Steve Nance, who was able to help put my thoughts and passion onto the printed page, while fighting some pretty big battles of his own. And finally we would never have been able to do all these incredible outreach ministries at Rock City Church in Baltimore without the awesome group of people who make up our church and who share a heart to go after the lost and hurting of our city.

Endorsements

"This book will rip your heart out! Rarely have I seen authentic compassion, the power and the presence of God, and integrity wedded together in one package. But that is exactly what I have found at Rock City Church in Baltimore—contagious, authentic Christianity under the leadership of Bart Pierce. Read this book and you will be moved to action!"

Jim W. Goll
Ministry to the Nations
Author, *The Lost Art of Intercession*
and *Father Forgive Us!*

"I don't know anyone who has as big a heart for the 'outcast' as Bart Pierce. The character of Jesus is truly his example! His compassionate and nurturing nature is seen throughout the pages of this book. *Seeking Our Brothers* is one of the most excellent writings of its kind, conveying the harsh realities of life while also providing practical solutions. I highly recommend it. Your heart will be moved to reach out to your community like never before!"

Dr. Kingsley A. Fletcher
Senior Pastor
Life Community Church

"Yes, Yes, and Yes! Bart Pierce has captured the very heart of God in his book, *Seeking Our Brothers*. Reading through the pages I could hear the prayer of Bob Pierce (founder of World Vision), 'God, break my heart with the things that break Yours.' I could hear the heart cry of praying John Hyde, 'Give me souls or I die.'

"Truly, Bart Pierce understands the need to go beyond mere declarations and proclamations by challenging the Church to go into action. John R. Mott, the 1946 Nobel Peace Prize recipient, once said, 'Evangelism without social work is deficient; social work without evangelism is impotent.'

"Bart is not merely a theorist, but a true practitioner. He exemplifies a cohesive leader who understands unity with a *soul* purpose.

"Bart Pierce through his book, *Seeking Our Brothers*, has laid a foundational blueprint for an outpouring of God's Spirit—ultimately touching hearts and changing cities."

Dr. J. Doug Stringer
Founder
Somebody Cares/Turning Point International

"Bart Pierce is one of those unique leaders who sees the need and then creates ways to meet the need. *Seeking Our Brothers* is about a church that believes in changing their city one person at a time. Buckle up: the ride is not your normal cruise along church. It is challenging, convicting, and heart-moving. It is a book that will change the way you do church!"

Frank Damazio
Pastor, City Bible Church
Portland, Oregon

"From a druggie to city transformer—what a leap! Bart Pierce has gone from the pit to helping change a whole city. If you are looking to transform your city, this is one of the most practical, insightful books you could own. I highly recommend it."

Cindy Jacobs
Co-founder, Generals of Intercession

Contents

Foreword

had the privilege of working closely with my good friend Pastor Bart Pierce in Baltimore for more than three years. Early in our relationship, it became obvious that the grace of God's presence hung heavy over services at Rock City Church. I remember one night puzzling over this in Bart's den. We realized that what was happening in Baltimore was unique because it combined intense, passionate worship with intense, passionate social outreach. He asked the question, "How can we convey that to the people?" As if by revelation it came to me:

Jesus loved both Mary and Martha. These two sisters hosted Jesus in their home, and the Scriptures give us detailed accounts of two of those visits. Mary was a worshiper—most suppose that this is the very same Mary who broke the alabaster box on Jesus' feet and wiped them with her hair. Martha was a servant—she is the one who looked after Jesus' practical and physical needs. In John 11:5 we're told that Jesus loved Martha *and her sister*—in this instance, Jesus Himself gives special attention to Martha.

Often we look down on Martha, but we forget that Jesus valued her contribution as well. We talk about Mary to the exclusion of Martha, but Jesus didn't see it that way. Jesus knew that when He visited their home, both the physical hunger of His humanity and the spiritual hunger of His deity would be satisfied. The combination of Martha and Mary, servant and worshiper, made their home a unique environment that Jesus wanted to visit. We can learn a lesson from these sisters. If we want our churches and our homes to be places that God wants to visit, we need to learn to host both the human and the divine.

We tend to focus on being one or the other—Martha or Mary—and our churches reflect this. As a result, we see groups who do an excellent job of hosting men and caring for man's needs, but lack dynamic, intimate worship. On the other side of the spectrum we see churches that are so heavenly minded they're no earthly good: they focus on worship, but neglect the needs of the people in their community. There are very few churches that effectively combine both the heart of Martha and the heart of Mary. (This is so important that I'm currently writing a book on this subject, to be released in July of 2001.)

I may be "Mary" by nature, but that doesn't completely relieve me of "Martha" duties. Bart Pierce may be "Martha" by nature, but as the passion of this book reveals, he also knows what it is like to worship at Jesus' feet. There is a little bit of Martha and a little bit of Mary in both of us.

This book will help you raise your credibility in the human realm. It is a manual for "Marthas."

—Tommy Tenney
Author, GodChaser

Introduction

Seeking Our Brothers tells the story of a body of people who are united by a vision and driven by a passion—through deeds of kindness—to reach a city. It is my belief that the Kingdom of God can
be established through the life of believers to affect, and ultimately transform, every part of society. We must, as Christ's ambassadors of His love
and mercy, become our brothers' keepers.

The story of the Good Samaritan is one of my favorite stories in the
Bible (see Lk. 10:25-36). It illustrates Christ's passionate love for those
who have been rejected and cast away along life's roadside. Jesus represents the Good Samaritan in the story and the Church represents the
innkeeper. The Samaritan knew rejection, being despised by his own, yet
refused to go by the one on the roadside who was hurting and desperate. Even though he was on his way to his appointed destiny, he stopped
and got involved, taking the hurting man to an available inn.

When the Samaritan departed, he took out two denarii and gave
them to the innkeeper, saying to him, "Take care of him; and whatever
more you spend, when I come again, I will repay you" (Lk. 10:35b). Jesus
is telling us that if we will take care of the ones nobody wants, He will
provide everything we need to care for them.

Seeking Our Brothers

My prayer is that every church throughout this nation and world will begin to see themselves as the innkeepers, and will get ready and make room for those whom our Good Samaritan (Jesus) is bringing from every walk of society. They are lying on park benches, back alleys, and crack houses all over our cities, right at this very moment.

As you read this book, may God fan the flame of your heart and compel you to pursue a life of compassionate Christianity.

From an innkeeper,
Bart Pierce

Chapter One

Unto the Least of These

And the King shall answer and say unto them, Verily I say unto you, Inasmuch as ye have done it unto one of the least of these My brethren, ye have done it unto Me (Matthew 25:40 KJV).

Curtis was an alcoholic. In fact, he was probably the number one "wino" in Baltimore. On the winter Sunday morning when he showed up at Rock City Church no one was aware at first that a sovereign, God-ordained sequence of events was underway. Staggering into the sanctuary dressed in who knows how many layers of dirty, unkempt clothes, Curtis sat down near the back. Those seated closest to him promptly moved several feet further away, not because they resented his presence, but because of his smell. Curtis reeked of booze, the filth of the streets, and his own vomit, which covered the front of him. His teeth had rotted away. A little bottle of liquor was tucked into a pocket of his ragged vest.

How Curtis came to be at Rock City Church that morning was a story in itself. As he related it later, he was sleeping on a heater grate for warmth when he was roused by a "big man" (Curtis always believed it was an angel) who said to him, "Get up. You're going to Rock City Church." Curtis told him to get lost and rolled over to go back to sleep. The next thing he knew, he was standing in our parking lot.

1

Right in the middle of my sermon Curtis suddenly stood up and staggered to the entrance of the sanctuary where, in full view of the congregation he opened the door, drank the rest of his booze and smashed the bottle against the side of the steps. Then he came back in and sat down. Actually, the alcohol helped him a little bit. It calmed him down so he could sit up straight.

During the time of ministry after the sermon, Curtis came to the altar where I laid hands on him and prayed. God smote him and he went out under the Spirit and lay on the floor for a little while. When he sat up a few minutes later he turned in astonishment to a church member nearby and said, "What did that man do?" Curtis was completely, stone cold sober! Christ saved him, healed him, and transformed him that morning. We baptized him and cleaned him up. I got him a car, gave him a job as a janitor at the church, even had a set of false teeth made for him.

As it turned out, Curtis had at one time owned one of the largest dairy farms in Pennsylvania. He had a wife and children, and was prosperous. Alcohol had destroyed it all. He lost his farm and his family, and ended up as a homeless drunk wandering the streets of Baltimore. After Curtis met Christ, however, he was totally changed. His transformation was so complete that one day a lieutenant in the detective division of the Baltimore police department drove out just to see me and personally thank me for what had happened to Curtis. For years this lieutenant had helped Curtis at Christmas and other holidays. Sometimes he put Curtis in jail simply to give him a night off the street.

Curtis worked as our janitor for about a year. Then early one morning he died peacefully in his sleep. Those of us who knew and loved Curtis grieved at his passing, yet at the same time felt great comfort that he had died not as a lost, wasted drunk, but as a new man in Christ.

TAKING CARE OF THE "THROW-AWAYS"

Curtis is just one example of the hundreds of radically transformed lives that are represented in the congregation of Rock City Church in Baltimore, Maryland, which I have pastored since 1983. Our church is full of people whose lives today—my own among them—are testimonies and trophies to God's power and saving grace. In this we are seeing the fulfillment of a word the Lord gave to me not long after I came to Baltimore, and which became foundational for everything we have done as a church. He said to me, *"If you will take care of the ones nobody wants, I will give you the ones everybody is after."*

From the beginning we have built Rock City Church on the principle and perspective of reaching out to the hurting, the broken, the wounded, the discouraged, the abandoned, and the rejected—in short, those whom society has written off as outcasts and "throw-aways." Yet, among those outcasts is an entire generation of people who are true "diamonds in the rough," and who, given the right opportunity and the favor of God, rise to incredible heights and become great leaders. I have seen this happen time and time again.

Ours is an ethnically diverse congregation, and the personal backgrounds of the people are just as varied. Many, like myself, are former drug addicts and drug dealers. There are women who were once prostitutes and nude dancers until Jesus changed them. We have women who as young girls were so molested and sexually abused by their fathers, grandfathers, uncles, or brothers that they couldn't even speak when they came to the church. Today they are happily married with children of their own and have been totally transformed by the love of God. We even have men who were once contract killers for major drug lords in the city. Now they serve the Lord of lords and love God with all their hearts.

One of these, a young African-American man, was so full of joy that he was always crying and shouting in church. One Sunday morning I asked him to testify to everyone else why he was so happy. As he stood up and began to tell how Jesus had saved him and changed him, a young white man stood up in another part of the sanctuary and began to walk toward him. Ten or fifteen years earlier, the white man had been shot in the leg and the hip during a drug deal gone bad. The shooter, a black man, had never been caught. On this morning the white man recognized the black man as the one who had shot him so many years before. It looked as though a fight was brewing. Instead, there in front of the whole congregation, these two former enemies embraced, hugged each other, repented to each other, and were reconciled. Christ can tear down any man-made barrier. Of course, the whole incident totally "ruined" the rest of our service; there wasn't a dry eye in the house!

A MANDATE FROM JESUS

I am convinced that reaching out to society's "throw-aways," the outcasts, and the destitute, the "ones nobody wants," is fundamental to

3

the gospel. It is certainly a defining characteristic of genuine followers of Christ. Jesus Himself made this clear in the parable of the sheep and the goats.

> *And He will set the sheep on His right hand, but the goats on the left. Then the King will say to those on His right hand, "Come, you blessed of My Father, inherit the kingdom prepared for you from the foundation of the world: for I was hungry and you gave Me food; I was thirsty and you gave Me drink; I was a stranger and you took Me in; I was naked and you clothed Me; I was sick and you visited Me; I was in prison and you came to Me." Then the righteous will answer Him, saying, "Lord, when did we see You hungry and feed You, or thirsty and give You drink? When did we see You a stranger and take You in, or naked and clothe You? Or when did we see You sick, or in prison, and come to You?" And the King will answer and say to them, "Assuredly, I say to you, inasmuch as you did it to one of the least of these My brethren, you did it to Me"* (Matthew 25:33-40).

In the eyes of Jesus, ministering to the poor, needy, and destitute in His name is the same as ministering to Him. On the other hand, rejecting or ignoring the needy is the same as rejecting or ignoring Jesus (see Mt. 25:41-45). For those supposed followers who refused to show compassion, Jesus had only words of judgment: "Then He will also say to those on the left hand, 'Depart from Me, you cursed, into the everlasting fire prepared for the devil and his angels'...And these will go away into everlasting punishment, but the righteous into eternal life" (Mt. 25:41,46).

Make no mistake about it: This kind of ministry is tough and it can be messy. You can't reach out to someone like Curtis without getting your hands dirty. Sometimes it means providing a bath or helping someone find a job. Sometimes, as with Curtis, it even means a set of false teeth. Compassion ministry means doing whatever is necessary to meet the need, and that requires getting outside the four walls of the church building. We can't take care of the hurting and hungry in the carpeted convenience of our comfort zones. We cannot afford to wait for them to come to us; we must go to them.

Somehow much of the modern Church has gotten things turned around. Far too often we avoid or turn our backs on the needy and destitute because it *is* hard work and there is very little "glory" in it, at least by man's standards. It *is* not what the typical "ministry" today likes to do. Besides, ministering to the needy can be expensive. It can "drain" a church's "limited" resources on people who most likely will give little in return. For churches with such a mind-set this would be "pouring good money after bad." Yet we simply cannot ignore the example of Jesus Himself. If we are serious about calling ourselves disciples of Christ, then we must "put our money where our mouth is" with regard to reaching the needy.

By all accounts, Jesus spent much more time among the broken and hurting than He did in the synagogue, the local house of worship. In fact, on at least one occasion in His own hometown of Nazareth, Jesus was *thrown out of* the house of worship! Ironically, He had just finished publicly defining His mission in terms of ministering to the needy. Reading from the scroll of Isaiah, Jesus said,

> *The Spirit of the Lord is upon Me, because He has anointed Me to preach the gospel to the poor; He has sent Me to heal the broken-hearted, to proclaim liberty to the captives and recovery of sight to the blind, to set at liberty those who are oppressed; to proclaim the acceptable year of the Lord* (Luke 4:18-19).

He then proceeded to rebuke the people for their unbelief. Stung by Jesus' words, the others in the synagogue sought in anger to kill Him, but He walked away (see Lk. 4:20-30).

Jesus was neither afraid nor embarrassed to be seen in the company of the poor and the hungry, the sick and the destitute, or to be thought of as "a friend of tax collectors and sinners" (Lk. 7:34b). After all, that is why He came! "Those who are well have no need of a physician, but those who are sick. I did not come to call the righteous, but sinners, to repentance" (Mk. 2:17b). We have a mandate from Jesus, by His own words and example, to take care of society's "throw-aways."

A HEART FOR THE CITY

For over 16 years Rock City Church has been committed to reaching the city of Baltimore with the gospel of Jesus Christ. This is both my personal passion as pastor and the corporate passion of the congregation as a whole. Our vision is to reclaim the city from despair, spiritual blindness, and the stranglehold of the enemy. The name *Baltimore* means "circle of Baal" and is derived from the ancient pagan worship of the

Druids in pre-Christian England and Ireland. There is even a section of the city known as Druid Hill Park. We believe that God has planted our church in Baltimore to help release the city from satan's grip and open the way for God to pour out His blessing and reveal His glory.

Many churches and denominations have virtually given up trying to reach the cities of our nation. In effect, they have written off the cities, surrendering them to the gangs and the drugs, to crime, poverty, and hopelessness. I am convinced that God has a heart for the cities of the world because that is where so many people live. In fact, God's desire and intention to reach the cities is at the "heart" of the divine outpouring of grace, blessing, power, and glory that He is releasing in many parts of the world in our time.

By turning its back on the cities, much of the Church is now looking in the wrong places and has forgotten the example of Jesus. Jesus didn't go after the social "elite," the people with money or power or influence. He didn't pursue those who were "beautiful" in the eyes of the world. Instead, He sought out rough, dirty fishermen like Peter and Andrew, James and John, blind beggars like Bartimaeus, hated tax collectors like Matthew and Zacchaeus, and sick people like lepers and the woman who had been hemorrhaging for 12 years. Once He even revealed the nature of true worship, not to the priests at the temple, but to a woman of ill repute who had been married five times and even then was "shacking up" with a man. Jesus was constantly reaching out to the people that "polite" society considered unworthy of attention.

In the 14th chapter of Luke, Jesus tells the story of a man who gave a great banquet but when the time arrived, all the invited guests made excuses as to why they could not come.

> ...Then the master of the house, being angry, said to his servant, "Go out quickly into the streets and lanes of the city, and bring in here the poor and the maimed and the lame and the blind." And the servant said, "Master, it is done as you commanded, and still there is room." Then the master said to the servant, "Go out into the highways and hedges, and compel them to come in, that my house may be filled. For I say to you that none of those men who were invited shall taste my supper" (Luke 14:21-24).

As Christians we are called to go out "into the streets and lanes of the city" and "into the highways and hedges" to reach the lost, especially those whom society has written off. The tragedy is that too often the Church has written them off as well.

God's heart is to redeem, restore, and bless the cities, and we must learn to have the same heart. Instead, most of us look at our cities and curse them. We complain about traffic and crime and other problems; we condemn our cities; we do everything except bless them. In Jeremiah 29:7 God commanded the Israelites who had been carried into exile to "seek the peace of the city where I have caused you to be carried away captive, and pray to the Lord for it; for in its peace you will have peace." We may not be living in exile today, but our responsibility to pray for our cities remains. How we speak about our city and how faithful we are to pray for our city will have a direct bearing on the quality of life and peace in the city for ourselves and for everyone else. We must cultivate a heart of compassion for our cities, and that compassion must be born out of a personal and collective passion for the Person and presence of the Lord Jesus Christ and for His glory and honor to be revealed.

MINISTRIES OF COMPASSION

At Rock City Church we have cultivated a heart for the city of Baltimore. We bless Baltimore. We believe that Baltimore is one of several major American cities that God is turning around in preparation for releasing true revival fire. As a matter of fact, Rock City Church has been living in revival for over three years. It was not our doing. God sovereignly showed up in a big way in January 1997 and revolutionized our church. We have seen Him do in our congregation what we believe is a pattern for what He wants to do with the Church as a whole in the new century: a reunion of "Mary and Martha," a restoring to the Church of both *passion* for the Lord and *compassion* for the lost.

Reaching the down-and-out has been my passion ever since I was saved in 1972. I think this is only natural because I was a down-and-outer myself; I know how they think, feel, and live. Since 1983, when I came to Rock City Church as pastor, the church has initiated a number of different ministries of compassion to the people of Baltimore. God has blessed us and granted us incredible favor in the city, and these ministries have grown and prospered to a degree we never could have imagined when we began. Today they operate with the cooperation, support, and assistance of local businesses, local law enforcement agencies, government officials and agencies, and other local churches throughout the city.

These ministries are discussed in much greater depth in the chapters that follow and especially in the Appendixes, but here is a brief description of some of the things we are doing to reach the city of Baltimore:

- A Can Can Make a Difference. Beginning as an emphasis encouraging church members to bring a can of food every time they came to church, this ministry to feed the hungry has grown to a full-scale operation with its own warehouse and which moves millions of pounds of food a year. It assists the hungry not only in Baltimore but in several cities in several other states as well.

- Nehemiah House. Since its inception in January 1991, the Nehemiah House has assisted over 2,200 homeless men find Christ, get control of their lives, and make the transition from homelessness back into productive lives in the workplace and in society.

- The Hiding Place. This seven-bed facility provides a secure home environment for young women in crisis or facing pregnancy. The nine-month program includes spiritual counseling, instruction in life skills and domestic skills, pre-natal counseling, and education and employment assistance. Since 1985 over 500 young women have received help at The Hiding Place.

- Adopt-A-Block. This is a strategy to reclaim and restore the inner city block by block. A specific block or neighborhood is targeted, and a block party is held which focuses on meeting the diversified needs of the residents: spiritual, emotional, mental, physical, and economic.

PASSION PLUS COMPASSION

On the edge of the new millennium God is redefining His Church. Or perhaps He is simply reorienting us to the mission we have had all along: reaching the masses—reaching our cities—with the gospel. Therein lies the future and the hope of the Church. Therein lies the *passion* of the Church. We should be passionate about our Lord and compassionate toward others, especially the lost who need to know that Christ loves them and died for them.

Whenever Jesus visited Bethany, He always stayed at the home of Mary and Martha and their brother, Lazarus. Luke 10:38-42 describes one such visit where Martha scurried around trying to be a good hostess while her sister, Mary, simply sat at Jesus' feet, listening to Him. Martha ministered to Jesus' humanity, seeking to serve His physical needs. Mary, on the other hand, ministered to Jesus' divinity by seeking simply to be with Him. Martha had *compassion* for the man Jesus; Mary had a *passion* for the Person of the Son of God. Both are important.[1] The earliest Christians served the needs of others out of a compassion that was fueled by their passion for Christ.

Somewhere along the way in the history of the Church, the two have become separated. Most churches tend to focus on either one or the other, rarely both. Either they concentrate on "social ministry" with little passion or love for Christ, or they concentrate on being "spiritual" while neglecting the needy around them. The biblical pattern is *both* working together: ministries of *compassion* in the context of *passion* for the Person and presence of Christ. The revival that began at Rock City Church in January 1997 has deepened and enhanced our understanding both of the importance of our personal and corporate passion for Christ and the connection between that passion and compassionate ministry.

Ours has been a passionless Christianity for far too long. It was *passion* that drove Jesus to the cross. It was *compassion* that caused Him to see the multitudes as those who were "weary and scattered, like sheep having no shepherd" (Mt. 9:36b). He wept over the city of Jerusalem. We too must learn to weep over our cities. Our passionate love for the Lord should drive us to go to the kinds of people He went to, love them the way He did, and lead them into the Kingdom.

I believe that in our day God wants to reunite passion and compassion in our churches to reach the cities of our land. In 1991 the Lord began speaking to me about the life of Joseph in the Book of Genesis as a model for what He wants to do today. God placed Joseph in a strategic place to fulfill His divine purpose. Joseph endured much hardship and adversity along the way, but he loved God and enjoyed God's favor. God raised Joseph up to bring deliverance from famine for the whole nation of Egypt, the surrounding region, and especially for his own family. In the same way, I believe that today God is raising up a "Joseph Generation," a company of believers who will not be satisfied to do things the same old way but who, with a fresh passion for God, will look for new ways to fulfill the Great Commission. It will be a company that God places strategically to be used to bring redemption and deliverance to our cities and our nation.

God wants to reach the cities. He wants to touch the untouchables, love the unlovables, restore the broken, heal the sick, lift up the downtrodden. How do I know? First, I know because it is the pattern we see in the Scriptures. Second, it is the pattern I have seen countless times through my years as a pastor. Most of all, though, I know it because God reached out to *me*. When I was growing up and was into drugs and in trouble, everybody said I was no good—schoolteachers, bus drivers, neighbors. They all said I was a loser. Then God said, "I can use him." I know God wants to touch "the least of these" because I was one of them and He touched *me*. I know He wants to transform "the ones nobody wants" because I was one of them and He transformed *me*.

ENDNOTE

1. This is a topic that Tommy Tenney often preached at the Rock City Church. He is currently writing a book on this subject, to be released in July of 2001.

Chapter Two

Never Again Alone

Therefore, if anyone is in Christ, he is a new creation; old things have passed away; behold, all things have become new (2 Corinthians 5:17).

When I walked into Rock Church in Virginia Beach, Virginia, one Sunday morning in 1972, I was a desperate man. Against all expectations I found myself at the altar at the end of the service. There, with hair down to my shoulders, dope in my pocket, and a contract on my head, I gave my heart to Jesus. I said, "Jesus, I don't even know if You're real. God, I don't even know if You're hearing me, but whatever it is, do it today or I'm gone." I was not exaggerating my situation. If God had not changed me by His love that day, I probably would not be here today. How did I get to that spot? What happened to turn me into such a desperate young man?

SHAKING MY FIST AT GOD

The first half of my life growing up was pretty normal. My father had a successful career in the construction business and, as well as I can remember her, my mother was a great mom. Ours was not a Christian home, but it was stable, at least as far as I could tell as a young boy. We enjoyed the same types of things that most other families enjoyed and life was good. All of that changed when I was nine years old.

One evening my mother scolded me for something I had done and threatened to put me on restriction. In typical, overblown nine-year-old fashion I stormed angrily to my bedroom, thinking how much I hated my mom and how mean she was to me. I went to bed still simmering with anger and resentment.

In the middle of the night I was awakened suddenly. Mom was very sick. My sister and I were taken to our uncle's house while Dad rushed Mom to the hospital. I can still remember the following morning as Dad lay down on the bed with my sister and me at our uncle's house and tried to explain to us that our mother had died of blood poisoning during the night. I remember feeling totally confused, with no understanding at all of what was happening.

At that moment a huge, gaping hole opened up in my life and I felt myself being sucked into it with nothing to grab onto. Since no one in my family knew God, no one had any answers for me or could say anything to help ease the pain, the guilt, the anger, or the confusion that I felt. The first time I saw my mother lying in her casket, looking so stiff and unreal, the hole in my heart grew deeper and wider and I felt myself plummeting farther down into it.

On the day of the funeral, before leaving for the cemetery, I went out into the backyard by myself. Looking up at the sky I raised my arm and shook my fist at God. I didn't know for sure whether He even existed, but that didn't matter. I told God that I hated His guts and that if He ever came near me, I would punch His lights out. The funeral itself was horrible, but worse still was the emptiness afterwards of a home without a mother. I felt abandoned, so incredibly alone. I was hurting deeply and was very, very angry. There was no one to talk to, no one to help me work through my pain. My anger began to grow and grow and grow.

DOWNWARD SPIRAL

By the following school year I was getting into all sorts of trouble. The driver of my school bus threw me off the bus and told me that I would not be allowed to ride anymore. From that point on I was a continual problem both at school and in the neighborhood. In the fifth grade I was expelled from school for punching the principal in the stomach. I was boiling inside with anger and hurt, and there was no one to console me.

School became for me a place to hang out with friends, get into fights, make trouble, and meet girls. My grades got worse and worse, and so did my behavior, until I was an absolute disruption to everyone. It got to the point where the principals and teachers simply wanted me out of their school system. The more they opposed me, the more I opposed them. I became more and more belligerent. My life was in freefall—a downward spiral toward destruction.

My father tried to help. He wanted to fill the gaps in my life, but his work in the construction business demanded a great deal of his time and energy. Besides, he was also struggling with his own loneliness. His personal need for female companionship occupied his attention.

Eventually, my father met and married a woman who was quite a bit younger than he was. In fact, our new stepmother was not much older than my sister and me, and we never really gave her a chance. Here she was, barely mature herself, suddenly thrust into the role of trying to be a mother to two deeply hurting, troubled kids. None of us knew what to do with the situation. My father and I were at odds, struggling hard to have any kind of relationship at all. At one point he even threatened to send me to military school. I know that deep down he really loved me, but he was caught up in his own struggles. My sister was struggling, my stepmother was struggling, and I was struggling. Our home was highly dysfunctional, to say the least. It seemed as though no one understood, no one could help, and none of us knew where to turn for help.

After awhile, I found a couple of outlets that seemed to ease (or at least disguise) the pain and emptiness in my life. One of these was surfing. Living in a beach town, I had plenty of opportunity and incentive to learn the sport. I began to surf and skateboard all the time, and became really good at both. My other outlet was drugs. A young friend turned me on to pot when I was 13, and I liked the way it made me feel. I also began to drink. I kept getting into more and more trouble (if that was possible). I would sneak out at night and get drunk. I would go on dates and get in fights with other guys. I was always ready to fight at the drop of a hat. I was thrown out of school (again). I was arrested numerous times for misdemeanors. I broke into houses, and by the time I was 14 had stolen 22 cars. I had a police rap sheet a mile long. My life was careening wildly out of control.

ALONE AGAIN

As if things could get any worse, my life was wrenched apart again when I was 17. One afternoon my father picked me up after a football game and dropped me off at a friend's house for the night. I awoke the next morning to find a state trooper waiting to escort me home. Late the night before, my father had been eating and drinking alone in the kitchen. At some point he had choked on a piece of meat and dropped dead on the kitchen floor.

When I got home, everyone was crying and out of control. No one knew what to do or how to handle this latest tragedy. My stepmother and I had never been able to get along with each other, and on the day my dad died, she put me out of the house and told me to never come back. Suddenly, I was all alone again. The hole just kept getting deeper and deeper, and I had nothing to hang onto.

Drugs had progressively become a bigger and bigger part of my life. Having begun with pot, I moved on to LSD and other hallucinogens, and even started using cocaine. The more drugs I did, the more I wanted. Gradually, I became involved with people from all kinds of bad backgrounds. I had plenty of close calls. Many times I found myself sneaking out the back of a house as the police rushed in the front. It seemed only a matter of time until I would be caught.

During this time in my life I met my future wife, Coralee. The minute I saw her I knew that there was something different about her and that I wanted to be with her. We dated for a little while, and after I moved away we still kept in touch through letters. I even flew back from Florida to Virginia Beach to take her to her senior prom.

By the summer after my stepmother threw me out of the house, and with one year of high school left, I had decided to move to Cocoa Beach, Florida. I bought a car, loaded it with my clothes and my surfboards, and took off with a friend. We rented an apartment right on the beach. It seemed like the perfect setup: We could surf every day, do drugs, and go to school.

Surfing was still a big part of my life. I ran a surf shop for awhile and entered surfing contests, travelling up and down the East Coast. I enjoyed surfing and was good at it, but it could not fill the gaping hole in my heart. Neither could the drugs. Here I was, a "cool" surfer guy, all messed up on drugs. Once I fell in with some guys who were involved big-time in stealing credit cards. We stole a bunch of surfboards, threw them into a van and, with a stolen credit card, drove to California looking for the perfect wave. Once there, my new "friends" stole everything I owned and left me with nothing.

For awhile I lived it up on Sunset Strip with a stolen credit card, then eventually got involved with some museum owners who were selling huge volumes of drugs that they brought in from Mexico. They gave me money and fronted me with drugs to sell back home.

I began to fly all over the country with drugs stuffed into my suitcases and sewn into my jackets. I returned to Virginia Beach, where I continued to surf, sell drugs, and take drugs. I also got hooked up with some Colombians who set me up to sell drugs. I thought it was cool because it gave me lots of money and I didn't have to work. I was making tens of thousands of dollars. I could fly anywhere and buy anything I wanted.

The one thing that I remember about this time in my life—the one thing that really sticks out in my mind—is how completely alone I felt through it all. I really had nobody.

MAN ON THE RUN

By this time, the police were after me in a big way. They were determined to bust me for drug dealing. Once, they even released a man from jail and put him in a house as a deliberate plant, trying to nail me. I can't count the number of times I was picked up and taken to the police station. It seemed that I always had some excuse, some alibi, some way out. Nevertheless, I could hear the clock ticking; if something didn't change in my life, before long my luck would run out and I would be sent away to jail for a long time.

One night while I was lying in bed the thought came to me out of the clear blue to go to Puerto Rico. For a long time I had wanted to surf there, and many of my surfing friends had already moved there and were enjoying the big waves. I left the next morning. A friend drove me to the airport where, carrying my surfboards and a bunch of dope, I took off to Puerto Rico. That very night the police showed up and busted several of my friends; they also had a warrant for my arrest. Many of my friends spent several years in jail for possession of illegal drugs. Because the warrant against me was still active, I hid out in Puerto Rico for awhile.

Eventually, I returned to Virginia Beach, trying to keep a low profile because the police were still after me. They were not the only ones. Some time before, I had ripped off some really bad guys from New Jersey in a bad drug deal and they had put a contract on my head. The word on the street was that I was "dead meat."

One night during the summer of 1969 I was walking along a street in Virginia Beach with Coralee. She had remained my girlfriend through all my escapades, including my flight to Puerto Rico, and we were getting pretty serious. Suddenly two guys pulled up in a car and stopped next to us. The one on the passenger side laid a gun across the car door and said to me, "Get in or I'll blow your brains out right here!" I did as I was told and we sped off leaving Coralee behind. She didn't know what was happening.

They took me out on a country road, stood me up against a sign, and the guy with the gun pointed it at my forehead. At that point I just closed my eyes and thought, *This is it. I'm going to die right here.* I heard the shot, a deafening ringing in my ears. I waited, but nothing else happened. As I opened my eyes, the gun was pointed above my head. The gunman had deliberately shot the sign instead. Then he lowered the gun to my face and said, "Next time, I'll blow your brains out."

They threw me in the car, drove back to the beach, and pushed me out, warning me that if I said anything they would hunt me down and kill me. This close call really shook me up and made me think hard about my life. Once again I had that overwhelming feeling of being all alone.

SETTLING DOWN

Coralee and I were married on May 3, 1970. It almost didn't happen. The first time I asked her father for permission to marry her, he refused. Our lives could not have been more different. He was a career naval officer and I was basically a knucklehead and a bum. I had no steady job, yet I seemed to have plenty of money to spend. It was clear that I was involved in some kind of lifestyle that they wanted their daughter to have no part of.

The day I returned from Puerto Rico the first time, I discovered that Coralee was soon to leave for Rome, Italy, because the Navy was transferring her father there. I could hardly believe it. I was about to lose someone else that I cared about. That was the pattern of my life: It seemed that everyone I ever loved either died, left, or ended up in jail. Now Coralee was leaving.

We both wanted to marry, so I kept working on her father. I got my hair cut and went out and got a real job. Finally, he agreed to let us marry. Coralee's parents left for Rome only a couple of weeks after our wedding. We had told them that we were going to live in Virginia Beach, that I was going to work as the assistant manager of a store, and that we'd be fine. Shortly after they went overseas, however, we moved to Puerto Rico and spent the first year of our marriage as true "beach bums." We surfed, enjoyed life, and payed our rent and bought food with Coralee's unemployment benefits and the money I made selling drugs.

Even in the midst of the surfing and the drugs, I was desperately searching for something, for purpose and meaning to my life. I knew something had to change. Once, while in Puerto Rico before Coralee and I married, I had taken 12 doses of LSD just for the fun of it. I was stoned for days with no idea of where I was or what I was doing. During that time I had a vision or premonition that I was in a car wreck. As I lay there in the wreckage, faces appeared to me in the clouds and said that I needed to stop right now or I was going to end up dead. At the time I didn't know whether it was a drug-induced, psychedelic experience or something else, but it really shook me up.

After awhile we tired of the "beach bum" life and moved back to the United States. We settled down in Charlottesville, Virginia, where I got a construction job at a nuclear power plant. My father's name and reputation in the construction industry helped me land some good jobs. By this time, Coralee was pregnant with our first child, and she went to visit her family in Rome. I stayed home and worked hard, hoping to join her there in a few months.

CLOSE ENCOUNTERS OF THE DIVINE KIND

While Coralee was in Europe, I began to have a series of strange encounters. I was living at a boarding house in a small Virginia farming town, along with several other men. Although there were three beds in my room, I was the only occupant. The room was rather bare except for the picture hanging on one wall. It was a reproduction of a classic painting of Jesus praying in the Garden of Gethsemane with the moon shining through and reflecting off the large rock where He was kneeling. It was the only picture in the room and it made me nervous. No matter where I moved in that room, I felt as if that picture had eyes and was watching me.

Down the hall lived two older men who invited me to watch television with them one night. On the screen a preacher was pointing his finger and saying, "No matter where you are, no matter what problems you have, Jesus wants to come into your life. If you're involved in drugs and other things, He wants to save you." I thought, *Whoa! Is this guy talking to me?* I later found out that the TV preacher was Billy Graham.

When I realized that the two older men were getting ready to witness to me and that they wanted to pray with me and lead me to Jesus, I got real nervous and scared and quickly left the room. The only place I had to go was back to my room with its picture of Jesus that watched me everywhere I turned.

A week later my car broke down on the way home from Virginia Beach where I had gone to get some drugs. A young couple in a little Toyota picked me up. As soon as I crawled into the backseat, the girl turned around and began telling me about Jesus and how much He loved me, that He had a plan for my life and that He wanted to save me. This was more than I could handle. I asked them to stop the car, and I got out.

What was happening? All of a sudden it seemed as though everywhere I went someone was talking to me about God. I didn't know what to do. After I got home I called Coralee in Rome to tell her what was going on. Strangely enough, she began to tell me of similar encounters she was having. She had been all over Rome, and to the Vatican, and had visited St. Peter's Cathedral and the Sistine Chapel. She had seen all the great artwork about God and about the Bible everywhere around her. She was even reading a book about the Dead Sea Scrolls. Everywhere she went she was being confronted by something having to do with God. It seemed so strange, even scary, that although we were half a world apart, we were having similar experiences. Since I didn't understand what was happening, I asked her to come home.

When Coralee returned, I moved out of the boarding house and we rented a little trailer. I worked hard every day, and we tried to get ready for the arrival of our baby and to figure out what marriage and parenthood were all about.

People continued to witness to us wherever we went. One day in the grocery store, a tall, thin "hippie" with long hair, a beard, and overalls talked to us about Jesus and handed us a gospel tract. I thought, *I can't believe this; even "hippies" are sharing Jesus with me!*

INTO THE FOLD

One weekend while we were in the Richmond, Virginia area to attend a rock concert, Coralee and I learned from one of her friends about a new church nearby called Rock Church. At Coralee's suggestion we went there on Sunday morning. Outside of our wedding day, I had hardly ever been inside a church in my life, so I did not know what to expect. I was edgy, angry, and ready for anything. If anybody tried anything funny, such as hugging me or ragging me about my long hair, I was likely to punch his lights out, even in church. I was so naïve about church that I even went in with dope in my pockets; I didn't know any better.

I felt uncomfortable being there to start with, so it didn't help when a short, little man grabbed me in a big hug as soon as I walked in and started dancing around and telling me how much Jesus loved me. I couldn't punch him because he had my arms pinned down. Finally, we sat down near the back. The preacher was a short, energetic, somewhat chubby Puerto Rican, and what he said made no sense to me. I could not understand what he meant. All I knew was that the longer I sat there, the more uncomfortable I felt. Even before the service ended I had reached my limit. Coralee and I left.

We intended to drive away as soon as we could, but before we could leave, the entire congregation had come out into the field where we were parked. They conducted some kind of groundbreaking ceremony there with a lot of shouting and singing, raising of hands and talking in what sounded like gibberish to me. It was really strange. I desperately wanted to leave, but our car was surrounded by people, and some were actually leaning on it.

Finally, we were able to leave. On the way home I reached in my pocket, pulled out the dope, and threw it out the window. I told Coralee, "Something is weird. I don't know what it is, but I just feel like I need to get rid of this stuff." Something had happened to us that morning, but we didn't understand what it was. Coralee revealed to me that she had felt an urge to go to the front of the church when the minister started asking people to respond. I had no idea what that meant.

Shortly after this, we decided to move back to Virginia Beach. I knew I was running the risk of being arrested, but I felt it was time to come home. After the move, we visited Rock Church again. This time an usher led us to seats near the front. The same short, chubby Puerto Rican was preaching again, but this time his words hit right home with me. He kept talking about how he had been a drug addict and about all the prisons he'd been in, and all the things he'd gone through because of his addiction. All of a sudden, I could hear this guy talking right to me. I could relate to him, and I knew that he was talking about something real. My heart was pounding inside of me.

Until then, one of the things I never did was cry. After my mother died, and then my father, I became very hard; nothing could make me cry. Now, however, tears were in my eyes and pouring down my cheeks. When the preacher asked for anyone who wanted God to come into his heart, to come to the altar, I got up and ran. Little did I know, but Coralee went down the other side.

I gave my heart and life to the Lord that morning. After crying and weeping there on my knees before Him, I heard a voice inside me that I'd never heard before. He spoke the words, "I love you, and I will never leave you, nor will I ever forsake you." Can you imagine what those words meant to me? At that time in my life nearly everyone that I had ever loved had left me. Now, God Himself had assured me that He would never leave me. The loneliness that had been my constant companion all those years suddenly went away. *Never again would I be alone.*

HUNGRY FOR GOD

Before I left the church that morning, I was encouraged to start reading my Bible. I didn't even own a Bible, so I had to go to a bookstore and buy one. As I began to read it, God opened up His Word to me in an awesome way. The Bible was like no other book that I had ever

20

seen or read; it contained words that had life in them. Those words began to change my life.

I discovered that God was real and alive and that He really did have a plan for my life. The stories in the Bible left me in awe. They were better than the best book I had ever read or the best movie I had ever seen. I could hardly believe it, but every day got better and better. Each day was more exciting and more awesome than the day before. I knew that God had really touched me, and I was hungry to know His plan for me.

Only a few weeks after Coralee and I were saved, our daughter Rachel was born. We moved into an apartment and began working hard at being good parents. We wanted to raise our little girl in the ways of God. Just a few months before we had talked about how cool it would be for our kids to get stoned with us. Now we were going to church every Sunday and talked about how to "train up our child in the way she should go."

I couldn't believe how things were changing. Something inside me was constantly growing and crying out for more of God. We wanted to serve and made ourselves available to help in any way. The only thing I had to offer was experience in construction, in building, and in running heavy equipment. Before long I was helping the church build its different additions.

After another year our son Matthew was born. Our life was full: two children to raise and church meetings on Sunday mornings and evenings, and on Tuesday and Thursday nights. We got involved in everything we could and loved it.

God began to open up opportunities for me to share my testimony. Different people in the community who had known me in the past heard that I had gotten saved. The bus driver who had kicked me off her school bus so many years before came to the church one day to find out if what she had heard about me was true. She wept openly in my office when she found out that I was indeed a Christian.

On another occasion a man came to the church who had lived down the street from me when I was growing up. I used to steal the milk off his front porch and had gotten into many fights with his sons. He ended up staying and became one of the head elders of Rock Church.

One night when I was testifying in the service, a police officer who had known me in earlier years was present. When he heard how God had changed me, he gave his heart to the Lord. God was really moving in my life. It seemed as though everywhere I turned I was running into somebody I had known before.

I was teaching a class at the church one night when my ninth grade science teacher showed up. I thought he was going to fall out of his chair when it dawned on him who I was! After the class he and I hugged each other. I think I was as amazed as he was. Years earlier he had thrown me out of his classroom, and now I was teaching him about God! Only the Lord could bring about such a transformation.

A NEW DIRECTION

As God revealed Himself more and more to me, He began to use me in awesome ways I never could have imagined. I found myself witnessing to people at work and saw many get saved. A passion began to grow in me for doing more than just going to church and helping out. I wanted this to be my life. I wanted to share God with people, to tell how He had changed me and how He could change them too.

Coralee and I moved into the church's halfway house and ran it for two and a half years. At times we had as many as 20 men at the house: druggies, alcoholics, mixed up, messed up guys. We poured our hearts out to them and loved them. Sometimes we had to deal tough with them and shake them. All the time that I was dealing with them, God was dealing with me.

After we left the halfway house, we got involved with the youth. As the youth pastors of the church we were responsible for hundreds of kids. We loved them and poured our hearts into them and watched with joy and excitement as many of them were saved and baptized. For years we ran a youth camp for these kids every summer and saw them meet God in the most incredible ways.

In 1980 God opened the door for me to serve as the national youth coordinator for "Washington for Jesus." We rented RFK stadium in Washington, DC, and over 33,000 kids showed up for the all-night event—one of the largest Christian concerts that had ever been held in the United States up to that time.

The desire continued to grow in my heart to be used by God and to be involved in what He was involved in. I began to preach more and more and served as interim pastor for several churches in our fellowship that were struggling, in transition, and without full-time pastors. I loved them, worked with them, and helped them get their feet back on the ground. God had set the stage for a new assignment.

CALLED TO BALTIMORE

One day in 1981 Coralee, who is a great woman of prayer, came to me and said that the Lord had told her that we were going to Baltimore, Maryland. My immediate thought was, *Baltimore! There's nothing for me in Baltimore. I need to live on the water. I'm a surfer; that's what I do. I don't want to be in some inland city like Baltimore.* In my mind I simply dismissed the whole idea.

In the summer of 1982 I was invited to preach one Sunday for a tiny congregation in Baltimore. At that time the group was meeting in the basement of a house. Rather unexpectedly, I really enjoyed myself. I preached about God's desire to send revival to change the city and how He wanted to raise up a people who would be hungry for him and run after him. I began to speak prophetically to that group. Little did I know that I was prophesying my own destiny in that church. After the service my kids and I went to an Orioles game and had a great time. I went home with no intentions at all of moving to Baltimore.

Not long after that, a visiting prophet who was a frequent guest at our church approached me in the hallway and said, "Bart, I believe that God has revealed to me that you are going to go to Baltimore." Almost on the heels of that, my pastor and his wife shared with me their feelings and their sense that God might want to send us to Baltimore. It was undeniable confirmation: First, Coralee received the word in prayer, then the prophetic flow that summer Sunday when I preached in Baltimore, then the word of the visiting prophet, and finally the word from my own pastor and his wife.

Coralee, the kids, and I moved to Baltimore on September 3, 1983. I preached the first Sunday after our arrival and we began to get settled into life in the big city. In no time at all God wrought an incredible miracle as He knit our hearts to that great city and its people. I sensed now that my destiny was woven into the very fiber of that city. I knew that this was God's plan.

In the beginning I did not understand all that would unfold in the days before us or the dynamics of what God would do through the years. My prayer from the start was, "Lord, give me the portion that is mine in this city." Since that day, there has been an incredible, ongoing miracle, something that only God Himself could have done.

Only God could take a drug addict like me, a nobody, a "throw-away," someone that nobody wanted, someone filled with anger, hurt, and bitterness, and turn him around completely, transforming him into someone that God could use in the work of His Kingdom. The very things that I had always said I would enjoy for the rest of my life—drugs and surfing—meant nothing to me anymore. The only thing that mattered was loving God with all my heart and living a life pleasing to Him. For me, that meant devoting myself body, mind, and spirit to building and leading a church that would be committed to reaching our city for Christ. Reaching the cities is at the very heart of God's purpose.

Chapter Three

Restoring Our Cities

Also, seek the peace and prosperity of the city to which I have carried you into exile. Pray to the Lord for it, because if it prospers, you too will prosper (Jeremiah 29:7 NIV).

Some years after I came to Rock City Church as pastor, a woman complained to me about why the church always had to be so involved in trying to reach the city. After all, it required so much time and hard work. Apparently, her ideal picture of church was to settle back and rest in comfortable middle class suburbia in a warm sanctuary with padded pews. Our idea of church was not the same as hers, and today she sits in her little country church with her little comfy folks doing her little cozy things.

Now don't misunderstand me. There's nothing wrong with suburbia, a warm sanctuary with padded pews, or with being country, comfy, and cozy. People living in the suburbs and in the country need the Lord too. The problem comes when any church—whether urban, suburban, or rural—focuses on its own comfort and convenience while losing sight of the lost and hurting people within its shadow. God has called us to much more than that. When we focus primarily on ourselves, we fail to fulfill the Lord's primary purpose for His Church: to reach lost people with the saving gospel of Jesus Christ.

Unfortunately, this woman's attitude reflects that of many church people all across our land today. Over the last half century or so churches by the hundreds have fled the cities for the suburbs, and many of those that have remained in the cities have adopted a "circle the wagons" defensive posture in a desperate attempt simply to hang on. Under the onslaught of an increasingly hostile and paganized culture, many churches have retreated inside their four walls and essentially given up any attempt to engage that culture with the bold truth of the gospel.

This isolationism of the modern Church, while nothing new, is nevertheless contrary to both the purpose of God and the practice of the New Testament Church. In the space of one generation the early Church turned its world upside down with the gospel. At great personal cost and sacrifice, but with incredible demonstrations of spiritual power and authority, those early believers transformed their culture to a degree that has never been repeated. Over the centuries since, much of the Church has gotten things twisted and backward. Today, instead of boldly and prophetically confronting popular culture and society with the truths of God, the Church by and large has become ineffectual at best and, at worst, made its peace with the world.

If our cities are to be restored, then the Church *must* be restored first. We must return to the Lord's original purpose and design to reach out to the lost and to touch the untouchables. We must regain our perspective of knowing the heart of God and having the mind of Christ.

GOD'S HEART FOR THE CITIES

The Scriptures make it clear that God desires for all people everywhere to know Him and receive eternal life. "For God so loved the world that He gave His only begotten Son, that whoever believes in Him should not perish but have everlasting life" (Jn. 3:16). "[God] desires all men to be saved and to come to the knowledge of the truth" (1 Tim. 2:4). "The Lord is not slack concerning His promise, as some count slackness, but is longsuffering toward us, not willing that any should perish but that all should come to repentance" (2 Pet. 3:9). God longs for people to turn to Him in faith. He would much rather save sinners who repent than see them die in their sins. "Say to them: 'As I live,' says the Lord God, 'I have no pleasure in the death of the wicked, but that the wicked turn from his way and live. Turn, turn from your evil ways! For why should you die, O house of Israel?' " (Ezek. 33:11)

God wants to restore our cities because He loves people, and cities are where most people are found. One of the clearest examples of God's heart for the cities is found in the Book of Jonah. God commanded Jonah to go to the "great city" of Nineveh and prophesy His judgment on its people because of their wickedness. Jonah's message was simple: "Yet forty days, and Nineveh shall be overthrown!" (Jon. 3:4b) When the entire city repented and turned to God, however, He spared them. "Then God saw their works, that they turned from their evil way; and God relented from the disaster that He had said He would bring upon them, and He did not do it" (Jon. 3:10). Then, gently chiding the grumbling Jonah, who was upset that the traditional enemy of his people had been spared, God said, "And should I not pity Nineveh, that great city, in which are more than one hundred and twenty thousand persons who cannot discern between their right hand and their left; and much livestock?" (Jon. 4:11)

Jesus exhibited similar compassion toward the people and cities of His day. Once, after preaching, teaching, and healing in Capernaum, and when the people of the city tried to keep Him from leaving them, Jesus said, "I must preach the kingdom of God to the other cities also, because for this purpose I have been sent" (Lk. 4:43b). On another occasion, Jesus lamented over the unbelief of the people He had come to save. "O Jerusalem, Jerusalem, the one who kills the prophets and stones those who are sent to her! How often I wanted to gather your children together, as a hen gathers her chicks under her wings, but you were not willing!" (Mt. 23:37)

The apostle Paul said that as believers "we have the mind of Christ" (1 Cor. 2:16b). In his letter to the Philippians he said that we should have the same mind that was in Christ, who willingly became an obedient servant in order to make salvation possible (see Phil. 2:5-11). In a like manner, we should have a servant's heart, giving sacrificially of ourselves and our resources in order to bring people to Christ. We have to go where the people are, and most of the people are in the cities.

Reaching the cities was a key strategy for the New Testament Church in fulfilling the Great Commission. For example, Paul's preaching and missionary efforts targeted the great cities of his day: Corinth, Philippi, Ephesus, Thessalonica, Berea, Athens, and Rome. The churches in Jerusalem, Antioch, and Ephesus all became centers for missionary outreach to the surrounding regions. The gospel spread throughout the Roman Empire during the first century as believers carried the message *from city to city*. Two thousand years later the strategy is the same: It is by reaching the *cities* that the Church will reach the *world*.

GETTING OUR SPIRITUAL HOUSE IN ORDER

Before our cities can be restored, our churches must be restored. We must get our spiritual houses in order and realign ourselves with God's purpose and plan. According to Second Chronicles 29–30, King Hezekiah's plan was to rebuild the temple *first*, then to reach the leaders and people of the cities. I believe this is what lies behind the current wave of renewal and the fresh outpouring of God's Spirit that we are witnessing all over the world in these days. Since January 1997, we have seen it happening at Rock City Church.

The 58th chapter of Isaiah reveals God's perspective on the restoration of His people and the relationship this has with reaching and restoring the cities.

> *"Shout it aloud, do not hold back. Raise your voice like a trumpet. Declare to My people their rebellion and to the house of Jacob their sins"* (Isaiah 58:1 NIV).

Even though these words were addressed to the nation of Israel, they also speak to us as the people of God. Israel's purpose in God's plan was to be a holy nation through whom the whole world would be brought back to Him. This did not happen, however, because the nation of Israel fell into sin and walked in rebellion and disobedience. Notice that God directs His words to *His people*: "Declare to *My* people their *rebellion* and to the house of Jacob their *sins*." He gets very personal here. He is talking about you and me and everyone who claims His name.

The uncomfortable truth that we have to accept is that when things are wrong in the land, the first place to look for the source of the problem is with the *people of God*. That's what these verses mean. Jesus said that we are the salt of the earth and the light of the world (see Mt. 5:13-14). If we are out of order, how can we expect our land to be in order? God's Word reveals what we must do. "If My people who are called by My name will humble themselves, and pray and seek My face, and turn from their wicked ways, then I will hear from heaven, and will forgive their sin and heal their land" (2 Chron. 7:14). The land will be healed when the *people of God* humble themselves, repent, and turn to God in prayer!

This is so important for us to understand today because our nation is in deep, deep trouble. America has gone completely "bonkers." The fabric of our society is unraveling and the edges are so frayed that, by ourselves, we cannot glue them back together. When we look for the reasons and the solution, we need look no further than the Church. Now don't get me wrong. One of the reasons our country is in such trouble is because most Americans don't know the Lord. But whose fault is that? By and large, the Church has done a poor job of holding up before the lost a strong, bold, consistent, and uncompromising witness to Christ.

As Christians we should look first to ourselves—to the Church—to understand why our nation is in trouble. We shouldn't be too quick to blame the government or our leaders. For example, inflation, recession, and other economic problems are not the result of "bad government" as much as they are the result of poor stewardship by God's people. Across the board, only 22 percent of church members tithe or give regularly to their church and to the Lord's work. When the Church isn't prospering, how can we expect the nation to prosper? We wonder why there are thieves in government. Well, there are thieves in the Church. The prophet Malachi wrote, "Will a man rob God? Yet you have robbed Me! But you say, 'In what way have we robbed You?' In tithes and offerings" (Mal. 3:8). Why are we surprised to find crooks on every street corner? If crooks can be found in the Church, they can be found anywhere. How can we expect to save our cities when so many of our churches are spiritually bankrupt and morally corrupt?

Poverty is not the result of bad social policy; crime is not the result of inadequate law enforcement. These problems are by-products of the lack of spiritual and moral standards in so many American homes and families today. So many Americans have lost their anchor and are adrift spiritually and morally, and the Church bears much of the responsibility.

The Lord is determined to get His house in order. When He comes in His manifested glory, He brings both correction and renewal, but He doesn't want His presence to stay confined within the walls of His house. He wants us to take it out into the cities. Second Samuel chapter 6 tells us that King David recognized his responsibility for the failed attempt to return the ark of God to Jerusalem, and he was afraid. He said, "How can the ark of the Lord come to [Jerusalem]?" (2 Sam. 6:9b) So David left the ark at the house of a man named Obed-Edom. After the ark had been there for three months, David heard that the Lord had blessed Obed-Edom and all his household while the ark stayed with them. That box didn't just sit there as a piece of furniture; it transformed the entire house. Scripture tells us that all eight of Obed's sons ended up becoming porters in the house of his God (see 1 Chron. 26:1-4). They became those who ushered in the ark of God and ushered the people to come to worship in David's tabernacle. Obed-Edom himself became a worship leader after the ark had been in his house (see 1 Chron. 15:18; 16:5).

But when David returned for that ark, Obed-Edom let it go with joy. He knew that God's glory was not meant to be just in his house, but was meant to be in the city.

What has God been doing for three years with us at Rock City Church? God has let us keep the ark. God has been changing us. But now it's time to carry the ark back into the city. It's time to carry it back into the schools and back into the marketplaces. It's time to carry it back into the alleyways, and carry it back through the streets of Jerusalem. It's time to walk down the street—back to Israel, the city of David. It's time to carry it back into the city.

Church, it's time to get our spiritual house in order!

LET'S GET REAL!

For day after day they seek Me out; they seem eager to know My ways, as if they were a nation that does what is right and has not forsaken the commands of its God. They ask Me for just decisions and seem eager for God to come near them. "Why have we fasted," they say, "and You have not seen it? Why have we humbled ourselves, and You have not noticed?" Yet on the day of your fasting, you do as you please and exploit all your workers. Your fasting ends in quarreling and strife, and in striking each other with wicked fists. You cannot fast as you do today and expect your voice to be heard on high. Is this the kind of fast I have chosen, only a day for a man to humble himself? Is it only for bowing one's head like a reed and for lying on sackcloth and ashes? Is that what you call a fast, a day acceptable to the Lord? (Isaiah 58:2-5 NIV)

The Lord's charge against His people was that they had made a *game* out of worship. They acted and sounded pious and religious, as if they were really interested in hearing from God and seeing His glory in their midst. In reality, however, their hearts were not yielded to Him. What they *said* and what they *did* were two different things. Their "worship" was just for show, and God wasn't fooled for a moment. Their "fast" consisted of dead ritual and empty words while God was looking for hearts consecrated totally to Him and His purposes. That is why He told them, "You cannot fast as you do today and expect your voice to be heard on high."

God's warning to His people in Isaiah's day is a message we need to hear and heed today. So often we come to church and display our "piety" and our "humility." We go through our routines of praise and worship; we sing our hallelujahs and say all the right things, but our hearts are far from God. Throughout our land, all over our cities, hundreds of churches every week go through the empty routine of "having church" with "a form of godliness" that denies its power (see 2 Tim. 3:5). We act and sound very "religious" and committed while we are in church, but walk away afterward with no intention of following through with the things we told God we would do. Instead, we continue to do just as we please.

To make matters worse, after all our pious posturing on Sunday, we rise up during the week to quarrel and fight among ourselves, or with our neighbor, or with the church down the street. The gangs in the street aren't as vicious as the gangs in the Church. At least the gangs in the street meet one another face to face. In the Church they operate undercover by phone, by letter, and behind the back.

No wonder we can't find revival! No wonder our cities are decaying and falling apart before our eyes! No wonder our cities can't find healing!

It's time for us to get real with the things of God! It's time to return to God and get back to worshiping Him in spirit and in truth! It's time to recapture our passion for Jesus and renew our compassion for the lost and the dying, the broken and the hurting who live in the shadows of our church buildings.

THE FAST THAT GOD CHOOSES

Is not this the kind of fasting I have chosen: to loose the chains of injustice and untie the cords of the yoke, to set the oppressed free and break every yoke? Is it not to share your food with the hungry and to provide the poor wanderer with shelter—when you see the naked, to clothe him, and not to turn away from your own flesh and blood? Then your light will break forth like the dawn, and your healing will quickly appear; then your righteousness will go before you, and the glory of the Lord will be your rear guard. Then you will call, and the Lord will answer; you will cry for help, and He will say: Here am I. If you do away with the yoke of oppression, with the pointing finger and malicious talk, and if you spend yourselves in behalf of the hungry and satisfy the needs of the oppressed, then your light will rise in the darkness, and your night will become like the noonday (Isaiah 58:6-10 NIV).

If we want God to hear us and act in our midst, then we must lay aside the "religious" fast of our own and take up the fast that *God* has chosen. He reveals plainly in these verses what that fast is: seek justice, free the oppressed, break every yoke of bondage, feed the hungry, shelter the homeless, and clothe the naked. This is a God-given responsibility that He has charged to His people. In the context of proclaiming the gospel to the lost we are to demonstrate the love and presence of the Lord through acts of compassionate ministry and service to the oppressed and needy.

Look at the powerful promises God has for us when we obey Him and take up the fast He has chosen: healing, righteousness, the light and glory of His presence, and the assurance that He will hear and answer our prayers! These are the qualities and characteristics of a Church that is walking in power, living in victory, and impacting a godless culture with divine truth. (I believe that because at Rock City Church we have been following the pattern of Isaiah 58, the glory of His presence came in our midst in January 1997.)

The condition for receiving these promises is to "do away with the yoke of oppression, with the pointing finger and malicious talk." Besides being ungodly, these activities drive away our sense of passion for the Lord and distract us from the ministries of compassion He has placed in our charge. How can we care for others when we are fighting among ourselves? How can we be spiritually free if we are under the oppressive yoke of "religion"?

The spirit of religion has brought great bondage into the Church. When we lack God's power in our lives and churches, we tend to turn to rules, regulations, and rituals. That's where legalism comes in. "Religion" and legalism never bring revival. Neither do they bring healing, either to the church or to the city.

While we sit in our churches having our "religious" parties, outside the four walls lost and needy people are groaning and crying for the mature sons of God to be manifested. If we would spend our time on the fast that God has chosen—reaching out to the lost, the poor, the hurting, and the needy all around us in our cities—we would have no time to waste on self-centered and sectarian "religious" activities that really have nothing to do with the Spirit, presence, or purpose of God.

RENEWED TO REBUILD AND RESTORE

The Lord will guide you always; He will satisfy your needs in a sun-scorched land and will strengthen your frame. You will be like a well-watered garden, like a spring whose waters never fail. Your people will rebuild the ancient ruins and will raise up the age-old foundations; you will be called Repairer of Broken Walls, Restorer of Streets with Dwellings (Isaiah 58:11-12 NIV).

Whenever we take on the fast that God chooses, we can depend on Him to sustain us. Anyone coming off a long fast is hungry; Jesus certainly was after His 40 days in the wilderness (see Lk. 4:2). Even a short fast with no water leaves one thirsty. Like a lost traveler stumbling through the desert (sun-scorched land) who needs to find an oasis or spring in order to survive, so we need God to guide us. That's the beautiful, refreshing promise of these verses. Just as a spring of water refreshes and renews the strength of a thirsty wanderer, so the Lord's guidance will satisfy our needs and strengthen our frame.

Furthermore, as we live and walk according to His will, we will find ourselves nourished and refreshed, like a "well-watered garden," no matter where we are. Like a "spring whose waters never fail," we will find God's sustaining grace, power, and resources with us all the time, and we will be continually renewed and refreshed with the strength to do what He has called us to do. He will take us into the places that we've only prayed about in our prayer closets. He will open doors, tear down walls, and bring us into a whole new walk with Him among those who have been rejected by everyone in the "religious" world. He will satisfy our needs because He is Jehovah Jireh (God the Provider). If we sow in the right field, we will reap the harvest of our cities.

I believe that's where God wants to bring us today. But He can't heal our cities until He heals His Church. We are in desperate need of healing. Sometimes the ground around us looks so dry and parched that we forget about the underground stream that supplies and sustains us. We are like trees firmly planted by rivers of water, bearing fruit in season, never withering, and prospering in every way (see Ps. 1:3). Sometimes we don't feel that way. That's when we need to remember to let our spiritual roots sink deep and tap into the perennially fresh water of God's sustaining grace and presence! After all, Jesus promised to give us water to drink that would never run out (see Jn. 4:13-14; 7:37-38). Once we tap into that fresh water, God wants us not to just "play in the river," but to let the river flow *through* us.

According to Isaiah 58:12, as children of God our purpose, our destiny in the Lord, is to "rebuild the ancient ruins," "raise up the age-old foundations," repair the "broken walls," and restore the "streets with dwellings." This restoration must occur in two dimensions: in the Church first, and then in the cities. Spiritual and scriptural foundations must be thoroughly restored in the Church before the walls and streets of the cities can be repaired (reclaimed). Politicians and government agencies do not have the answer to the restoration of the cities. The Church does; it is part of our commission from the Lord.

We need to return to the foundations of honesty, integrity, holiness, and righteous lifestyles. We need to reaffirm biblical order and values in our families with children respecting their parents, parents respecting their children, and with husbands and fathers fulfilling their God-given role as the spiritual head of the home. This is the kind of restoration that God wants. It must happen in the Church before we can expect it to happen in the streets and in the cities.

Make no mistake about it, we have our work cut out for us! There is no time to waste. We have done enough of that already, sitting on our padded pews, feasting and fellowshiping with saints at Sunday supper after service! It's high time for us to let our light shine once again—the light of the glory of God shining through us, which is the distinguishing mark of the saints of the Lord.

We don't need a special robe or a cross around our neck or a huge Bible under our arm to show the world that we are Christians. What we *do* need is Christ's robe of righteousness, personal repentance at the cross, and the Bible alive in our hearts. We need to let God arise and reign. We need to cry out in desperation for Him and get so hungry for Him that nothing else matters. When we get hungry and humble and holy, His glory will come. When His glory comes, His power will come. When His power comes, we will see His purpose accomplished in and through us. The people of our cities will see His light in us and will turn to Him, because He will draw them to Himself.

In our day God is raising up a generation of believers who will not be content simply to "do church" the old way, but who will be committed, in the power of the Spirit, to reaching the cities for Christ. I call this army of disciples the "Joseph generation," or "Joseph company," after the Old Testament patriarch Joseph, son of Jacob. Genesis chapters 37–50 relate the story of Joseph, who was sold into slavery by his brothers but rose to second in command in Egypt. God specifically and deliberately raised up Joseph and positioned him in Egypt to save and preserve not just his own family, or even a single city, but an entire nation.

Before we look at the characteristics of the "Joseph company" of our day, we need to examine the life of Joseph himself, and how God prepared and used Joseph to accomplish His divine purpose.

Chapter Four

Joseph: Dreamer of Dreamers

Then He said, "Hear now My words: If there is a prophet among you, I, the Lord, make Myself known to him in a vision; I speak to him in a dream" (Numbers 12:6).

The account of Joseph in the Book of Genesis is one of the most moving and powerful stories in the Bible. It has all the elements of a great tale: a likable hero, despicable villains, plenty of human drama, plot twists with sudden reversals of circumstances, an exotic setting, some romance, and a happy ending. More importantly, it is a story of faith, integrity, moral character, triumph over adversity, forgiveness, redemption, and the unfailing purpose of God.

Joseph's story is also one of the most historically verified accounts in the Old Testament. Ancient official Egyptian records have been found which make reference to the seven years of plenty and the seven years of famine that are so integral a part of the biblical narrative. So, as with anything in the Scriptures, when we read about Joseph, his father, and his brothers, his trials as a slave in Egypt, and his triumph as prime minister of Egypt, we are reading about real people and real events. Everything that happened, good or bad, served to realize God's purpose to build and preserve a nation and to fulfill the promises He made to Abraham, Isaac, and Jacob.

More space is given to Joseph than to any other person in the Book of Genesis, including Abraham. Joseph was a man whom God raised up at a specific time and in a specific place to fulfill a specific part of the divine plan. In Joseph and his experiences we can see a type and a foreshadowing of Christ. Clearly, then, this is a story to which God wants us to give special attention.

FAMILY TIES?

Joseph grew up in a family that we would describe today as dysfunctional. He and his 11 brothers had been born to four different women, all of whom were wives of his father, Jacob. Talk about a spirit of competition! Try to imagine the stress and jealousy that existed in that household! Two of Jacob's wives, Leah and Rachel, were sisters, and daughters of Jacob's uncle Laban. Rachel was Jacob's favorite, but she was barren for many years. Leah, on the other hand, bore Jacob six sons: Reuben, Simeon, Levi, Judah, Issachar, and Zebulun. When Rachel saw that she was barren, she gave her handmaid Bilhah to Jacob, who bore to him Dan and Naphtali. Not to be outdone, Leah gave her handmaid Zilpah to Jacob. Zilpah gave birth to Gad and Asher. Finally, after many years of prayer, Rachel herself gave birth to Joseph and, much later, to Benjamin (see Gen. 29:31–30:24; 35:16-18).

As if competition between Jacob's wives and sons was not bad enough already, Jacob made the situation worse by favoring Joseph above his other sons. Jacob loved Joseph more because he had been born to Jacob in his old age and because he was the son of Jacob's beloved wife, Rachel. Not surprisingly, this favoritism toward Joseph stirred up in his brothers intense envy and jealousy that eventually grew into a murderous hatred.

One day, when Joseph was 17, he was feeding the flock with his brothers. Benjamin, still too young to leave home, was not with them. Joseph's sibling problems were with all his *other* brothers. Apparently Joseph was shocked at their behavior. Maybe they were cussing and drinking or carousing with loose women. Whatever it was, "Joseph brought a bad report of them to his father" (Gen. 37:2b). He "tattled" on his brothers. Anyone who has younger siblings can remember what *that* was like growing up! An already bad situation grew worse. The fact that Jacob apparently rewarded Joseph by giving him a "coat of many colors" only added insult to injury (see Gen. 37:3). The brothers' hatred of

Joseph grew to such a degree that they "could not speak peaceably to him" (Gen. 37:4b).

Wait 'til I Tell You About the Dream I Had!

To top it off, Joseph received two prophetic dreams, which he promptly shared with his family. Whether he told his dreams matter-of-factly or with the brash boastfulness of youth the Scripture doesn't say. Regardless, Joseph's dreams drove the wedge deeper between him and his brothers.

> *Now Joseph had a dream, and he told it to his brothers; and they hated him even more. So he said to them, "Please hear this dream which I have dreamed: There we were, binding sheaves in the field. Then behold, my sheaf arose and also stood upright; and indeed your sheaves stood all around and bowed down to my sheaf." And his brothers said to him, "Shall you indeed reign over us? Or shall you indeed have dominion over us?" So they hated him even more for his dreams and for his words. Then he dreamed still another dream and told it to his brothers, and said, "Look, I have dreamed another dream. And this time, the sun, the moon, and the eleven stars bowed down to me." So he told it to his father and his brothers; and his father rebuked him and said to him, "What is this dream that you have dreamed? Shall your mother and I and your brothers indeed come to bow down to the earth before you?" And his brothers envied him, but his father kept the matter in mind* (Genesis 37:5-11).

Joseph was a dreamer. This was the first recorded manifestation of a spiritual gift that would play a significant role in Joseph's life from then on.

Exactly what Joseph thought of his dreams is not clear, but his brothers understood what they meant. The very idea that this young upstart, this hated "daddy's boy," would ever rule over them was utterly out of the question. These brothers were a vicious, jealous, unruly bunch. In an age when respect for parents was assumed, even Jacob had trouble controlling his boys. At one point Reuben, the eldest, slept with Bilhah, his father's concubine (see Gen. 35:22). On another occasion Judah, the fourth son of Leah, got Tamar, his own daughter-in-law, pregnant (see Gen. 38). Some years before this, Simeon and Levi had treacherously murdered every male in the city of Shechem in revenge for the rape of their sister Dinah by the son of the local ruler (see Gen. 34).

These sons of Jacob were not "nice boys." They were hard, ruthless men capable of callous and cruel acts, who rebelled against authority and basically did what they pleased. It was dangerous for Joseph to incur their wrath.

Even though Joseph's dreams got him in even deeper hot water with his brothers, those dreams revealed something of the purpose of God. First, God was establishing a new order. Before God ever does something on the earth, He always reveals to His people what He is about to do. He establishes *His* government and order before He pours out His anointing, so that His blessing comes on top of the government that He establishes. Although young Joseph had no way of knowing it at the time, God was preparing to use him to feed an entire nation, to provide for his father and his brothers, and to set the stage for the establishment of the nation of Israel. *Joseph was born at the right time and place to fulfill his role in God's plan.*

The second thing to realize from Joseph's dream is that the purpose of God is never limited to one individual person or group, but extends to the entire human race. Everything that God does toward man has a redemptive purpose, that we may turn to Him, know Him, and give Him glory. The Egyptians of Joseph's day did not know the true God, but would witness His power in Joseph's life and partake of the blessings God would pour out during a time of famine. Through it all God would be glorified.

AWAY WITH THE DREAMER!

The problem with dreamers is that often they aren't very popular. Many people reject the messages of God that come through the dreams of visionaries. Dreams themselves are invisible, intangible things. So instead of attacking the dream or its content, they attack the dreamer. Somehow they seem to think that if they can silence the visionary, then the vision will not come to pass. God-inspired visions, however, have a life of their own; their survival does not depend upon the survival of the visionary.

One day not long after Joseph had shared his dreams, his father sent him to check up on his brothers who were tending their flocks near Shechem, a good day or two away by foot. What was Jacob thinking? Surely he must have known how his older sons hated Joseph, particularly after the "bad report" he had given about them the last time. Had he no more regard for the safety of his favorite son than to send him out to check on his brothers after he'd already squealed on them once? In the world *I* grew up in, a "stool pigeon" usually ended up getting hurt *really* bad. Is it possible that Jacob simply never "dreamed" that anything would happen to his "darling" boy?

Many times dreamers and visionaries must learn to walk alone before they can walk together with their brothers. David learned to worship alone with only his father's sheep to hear, so that he could worship in the masses and even lead in worship without being distracted. Jesus often walked away from his brothers (the disciples) to pray privately, so He could then pray with five thousand on the side of a hill and not be distracted. Joseph had to learn the hard lesson of being alone so he could handle the pressure of ruling a nation. Today some of God's leaders spend more time with the crowds and less time alone with God. One day, standing on a rock at the edge of Lake Erie, I heard God asking me, "Will you still seek Me when others are seeking you?" Dreamers need time to be alone with only their dream and God the dream-giver.

Joseph's brothers saw him coming from a long way off and plotted to kill him. "Then they said to one another, 'Look, this dreamer is coming! Come therefore, let us now kill him and cast him into some pit; and we shall say, "Some wild beast has devoured him." We shall see what will become of his dreams!' " (Gen. 37:19-20) For some reason Reuben, the eldest, persuaded the others not to kill Joseph, but to put him into a pit— perhaps an empty cistern—instead. The Bible says that Reuben planned to rescue Joseph later and return him to his father. Why did Reuben show this sudden concern for Joseph? Perhaps it was because as the eldest son he felt a particular responsibility for the safety of all his brothers, even the despised Joseph. Certainly, God's hand was evident, protecting Joseph for the future, even if Reuben had no idea of the part he played.

Joseph's treacherous brothers threw him into the pit, then calmly sat down to enjoy a meal, ignoring the cries that certainly must have risen from their terrified younger brother. Men of opportunity that they were, they saw a chance to profit from Joseph's misfortune when some Ishmaelite traders passed by. For 20 shekels of silver they sold Joseph to the Ishmaelites, who in turn took Joseph to Egypt and sold him into slavery.

Thinking that they were rid of "the dreamer" at last, the brothers concocted a lie for their father. Dipping Joseph's beautiful coat in goat's blood, they then told Jacob that Joseph had been devoured by a wild beast. Apparently, Reuben was absent when Joseph was sold, because he was upset to find him gone. Nevertheless, it appears that he participated in the cover-up. Certainly, these were men of sterling character! What had they accomplished? They had gotten rid of Joseph (or so they thought), sent their father into perpetual mourning over him, and sowed in themselves seeds of guilt that would gnaw away for years at their black and hardened hearts. Meanwhile, God was at work in Egypt.

DOWN BUT NOT OUT

Somehow while he was growing up, Joseph avoided developing the bitterness, anger, and rebellion that characterized his older brothers. The Scriptures give no hint that Joseph ever harbored any animosity toward his brothers for what they had done to him. Instead, the story focuses on the Lord's presence with Joseph and how God caused him to prosper.

> *Now Joseph had been taken down to Egypt. And Potiphar, an officer of Pharaoh, captain of the guard, an Egyptian, bought him from the Ishmaelites who had taken him down there. The Lord was with Joseph, and he was a successful man; and he was in the house of his master the Egyptian. And his master saw that the Lord was with him and that the Lord made all he did to prosper in his hand. So Joseph found favor in his sight, and served him. Then he made him overseer of his house, and all that he had he put under his authority. So it was, from the time that he had made him overseer of his house and all that he had, that the Lord blessed the Egyptian's house for Joseph's sake; and the blessing of the Lord was on all that he had in the house and in the field* (Genesis 39:1-5).

The key to the amazing success and victory in Joseph's life is found in the first phrase of verse 2: "The Lord was with Joseph." This tells us at least two things. First, the hand of God was on Joseph in spite of the unexpected and unpleasant turn his life had taken. Sometimes it is hard to see the working of God in our lives when we are surrounded by negative circumstances. If we focus on those circumstances, we may miss seeing how God works to turn them to His purpose. Apparently Joseph had his focus in the right place. As he sought to honor God no matter where he was, God honored him and caused him to prosper.

Second, the phrase, "The Lord was with Joseph" tells us that *Joseph was a righteous man*. He knew God and sought to follow Him. Joseph entrusted his life and welfare to God's care and God took care of him. King David the psalmist wrote,

> *The eyes of the Lord are on the righteous, and His ears are open to their cry....The righteous cry out, and the Lord hears, and delivers them out of all their troubles....Many are the afflictions of the righteous, but the Lord delivers him out of them all* (Psalm 34:15,17,19).

Joseph became the slave of Potiphar, the captain of Pharaoh's guard, who was so impressed with Joseph's honesty, integrity, and character that he made Joseph the manager of all his affairs. "Joseph found favor in [Potiphar's] sight, and...the Lord blessed [Potiphar's] house for Joseph's sake." Even as a lowly slave Joseph displayed God-given qualities of leadership.

There is one thing for sure about righteous people: They draw attacks from the enemy like sugar draws flies. Joseph was no exception. Genesis 39:6 describes Joseph as "handsome in form and appearance." It wasn't long before he caught the lustful, roving eye of Potiphar's wife, who tried on numerous occasions to seduce him. Joseph's response to this temptation is further evidence of a righteous man whose heart and mind were in tune with God.

> *But he refused. "With me in charge," he told her, "my master does not concern himself with anything in the house; everything he owns he has entrusted to my care. No one is greater in this house than I am. My master has withheld nothing from me except you, because you are his wife. How then could I do such a wicked thing and sin against God?" And though she spoke to Joseph day after day, he refused to go to bed with her or even be with her"* (Genesis 39:8-10 NIV).

Joseph resisted her advances for two reasons: He refused to betray Potiphar's trust and, more importantly, he refused to sin against God. His integrity came at a price, however. After one particularly insistent attempt by Potiphar's wife to seduce Joseph, he fled, leaving his coat behind. It is one thing to lose your coat, but quite another thing to lose your character. That's when she turned the tables on him, claiming that *he* had seduced *her* and that *she* had resisted and cried out for help. As a result of this slander, Potiphar threw Joseph in the dungeon.

There is such a great need today for this kind of heart from God's leaders. Joseph was a leader being trained in God's school. The world buys its leaders; God makes His! For us to be used today by God to heal a nation and rescue our brothers and families, we must be men and women of integrity. We must be willing to keep our integrity at any cost—even if it means the loss of family, friends, or anyone!

Once again Joseph found himself in a tough spot. He was fast becoming a man who was *familiar with adversity*. First, his brothers had sold him into slavery. Now, after working long and hard to gain the trust of his master, here he was in prison, falsely accused and with his character impugned. It must have seemed that everything Joseph had worked for had come to nothing. He had reached the bottom. Or had he? Joseph was down but not out, because the Lord was still with him. He was just where God needed him to be in order for the next page of the divine plan to unfold.

FROM PRISON CELL TO PHARAOH'S COURT

It's said that you can't keep a good man down, and that was certainly true with Joseph. With God's favor upon him he prospered, even in prison. Joseph was like the man described by the psalmist: "But his delight is in the law of the Lord, and in His law he meditates day and night. He shall be like a tree planted by the rivers of water, that brings forth its fruit in its season, whose leaf also shall not wither; and whatever he does shall prosper" (Ps. 1:2-3). Before long, the prison warden had entrusted Joseph with the management of affairs inside the prison. All the other prisoners were in his charge.

One day a couple of high-profile prisoners arrived: the pharaoh's personal baker and butler, who had offended him somehow and were being punished with jail time. They were placed in Joseph's care. Not long after, both men had disturbing dreams on the same night—prophetic dreams that neither of them could understand. The next morning Joseph noticed that the two men were sad. When they told him that they could not understand their dreams, Joseph replied, "Do not interpretations belong to God? Tell them to me, please" (Gen. 40:8b).

Joseph was a man who was spiritually alert. He noticed the sadness of the butler and baker and assured them that God could interpret their dreams. Sure enough, as the two men related their dreams, the Lord imparted to Joseph the interpretations. The butler received good news: In three days Pharaoh would restore him to his former position. Joseph made a request of him. "But remember me when it is well with you, and please show kindness to me; make mention of me to Pharaoh, and get me out of this house. For indeed I was stolen away from the land of the Hebrews; and also I have done nothing here that they should put me into the dungeon" (Gen. 40:14-15). The baker was not so fortunate. His dream meant that in three days he would be hanged.

Joseph's interpretations of the dreams came true just as he had said. Three days later the baker was hanged but the butler was restored to his place of serving the pharaoh. However, perhaps in the joy of his restoration, the butler forgot Joseph's request.

Often in the journey to fulfill God's purpose in our lives, we will be used and then forgotten by the very ones we've blessed or helped. Jesus knew this kind of ingratitude in His ministry. (Only one of ten healed lepers returned to say thanks.) To be used today to be a deliverer, a city transformer, a pastor, or leader in God's Kingdom, you have to be willing to pour out what God gives you, expecting nothing in return.

Two years passed. Then one night Pharaoh himself received a pair of prophetic dreams that left him completely baffled and unsettled. In the first, seven fat healthy cows came out of the Nile River to feed in the meadow. After them came seven thin and ugly cows who ate up the healthy cows. The second dream was similar except that instead of cows, seven plump, healthy heads of grain were devoured by seven thin and blighted heads of grain (see Gen. 41:1-7).

Pharaoh had no idea what his dreams meant and none of his magicians or wise men could shed any light either. That's when Pharaoh's butler remembered Joseph. He explained to the king about his own dream while in prison and how Joseph had correctly interpreted it for him. Pharaoh immediately sent for Joseph. After shaving and changing his clothes, Joseph came before Pharaoh.

GOD'S MAN OF THE HOUR

There is always a set time for the outworking of God's plan and for the deliverance of His people. Joseph languished in prison for two years after Pharaoh's butler was released. Now the stage is set. Pharaoh needs someone to interpret his dreams. God's time has come. Joseph's hour has arrived, the hour for which God has been preparing him all his life. Being spiritually alert and sensitive, Joseph by this time was certainly aware that God was working in his life. Now he was prepared to interpret Pharaoh's dreams. The failure of Pharaoh's magicians and wise men to do so only heightened the magnitude of Joseph's accomplishment and clearly revealed the singular power of God.

> *And Pharaoh said to Joseph, "I have had a dream, and there is no one who can interpret it. But I have heard it said of you that you can understand a dream, to interpret it." So Joseph answered Pharaoh, saying, "It is not in me; God will give Pharaoh an answer of peace"* (Genesis 41:15-16).

Joseph's boldness before the king of Egypt is almost shocking. Pharaoh says, "Interpret my dream," and Joseph replies, "I can't." Can you imagine a slave telling a king "I can't"? *That's boldness!* Joseph was quick to add, however, that God would give the interpretation. Joseph used his first audience before Pharaoh to give glory to God. Can you imagine a foreign slave testifying to the power of his God before a pagan king? *That's boldness!*

As Pharaoh related his dreams God imparted their meaning to Joseph (see Gen. 41:25-32). The seven healthy cows and the seven healthy heads of grain represented the same thing: seven years of plenty. Likewise, the seven thin cows and seven blighted heads of grain together represented seven years of severe famine, which would follow the seven years of plenty. The famine would be the worst that anyone anywhere could remember. It would deplete the land and be so severe that the seven years of plenty preceding it would be forgotten. Then Joseph said, "And the dream was repeated to Pharaoh twice because the thing is established by God, and God will shortly bring it to pass" (Gen. 41:32).

At this point, Joseph's "holy boldness" asserted itself even further. There is no indication that Pharaoh asked Joseph for advice, but Joseph offered it anyway. Can you imagine a slave fresh from the dungeon giving counsel to the king? *That's boldness!* If you're always looking at your position or circumstances of life, you'll never rise up to the next level God has for you. The Scripture says, "The righteous are bold as a lion"

(Prov. 28:1b). Living righteously by faith will cause great boldness to come upon us for all of life's circumstances. We are called to be the head, not the tail. Perhaps Joseph discerned where God was going with all of this. At any rate, he advised the king,

> *Now therefore, let Pharaoh select a discerning and wise man, and set him over the land of Egypt. Let Pharaoh do this, and let him appoint officers over the land, to collect one-fifth of the produce of the land of Egypt in the seven plentiful years. And let them gather all the food of those good years that are coming, and store up grain under the authority of Pharaoh, and let them keep food in the cities. Then that food shall be as a reserve for the land for the seven years of famine which shall be in the land of Egypt, that the land may not perish during the famine* (Genesis 41:33-36).

Pharaoh was impressed. Joseph, the Hebrew slave, had not only explained the king's dreams but also shown him how to prepare his nation for the coming famine.

> *And Pharaoh said to his servants, "Can we find such a one as this, a man in whom is the Spirit of God?" Then Pharaoh said to Joseph, "Inasmuch as God has shown you all this, there is no one as discerning and wise as you. You shall be over my house, and all my people shall be ruled according to your word; only in regard to the throne will I be greater than you." And Pharaoh said to Joseph, "See, I have set you over all the land of Egypt"* (Genesis 41:38-41).

The moment had come. God's man was now in place. *Joseph was a person who enjoyed the favor of both God and men.* God's favor was always upon him. He had won the favor of Potiphar (losing it only after being falsely accused by Potiphar's wife). He had won the favor of the prison warden and of Pharaoh's butler. Now Joseph had won the favor of Pharaoh himself. In His perfect timing God had lifted Joseph up from a prisoner in a jail *in* Egypt to the prime minister *of* Egypt. If you'll be faithful to God's dream, there's no prison that can keep you from the fulfillment of that dream. Joseph's words, "What man meant for evil, God meant for good" (see Gen. 50:20) is the key that will unlock the doors of all the prisons of life. Not only your cell door will open, but like Paul and Silas all the prison doors will open—even your family's cell doors will open; even the city gates will open. Joseph had risen from obscurity as the eleventh son in a nomadic family to second in command of the most powerful nation in the world. He was now poised to fulfill his calling as a savior, of sorts, who would preserve entire nations during famine and bring reconciliation within his own family.

SEEKING HIS BROTHERS

During the seven years of plenty, Egyptian farmers saw bumper crops and bountiful harvests as never before. Under Joseph's capable administration the surplus was gathered into storehouses throughout the land and kept in reserve against the famine years that lay ahead.

Once the years of famine began and food ran out, Joseph opened the storehouses and sold grain to the Egyptians. He also sold grain to visitors from the surrounding nations that were also affected by the famine. Because of Joseph's careful preparation, there was more than enough for everyone.

One day Joseph received a tired, dusty party of ten men who had traveled to Egypt from the north in order to buy grain. As he looked them over, he could hardly believe his eyes. Their faces were older, more wrinkled and weather-beaten than he remembered, but there was no doubt. Standing before him were his ten brothers, the very same men who had sold him into slavery. Joseph had not seen them in over 20 years. Now, in fulfillment of his dream from so many years before, his brothers were bowing before him. Of course, they did not recognize him. How could they? The last they had seen of Joseph he was being dragged off in chains screaming and crying. As far as they knew, he was probably dead by now.

Joseph saw an opportunity to bring his entire family back together and protect them during the famine. This was also part of God's plan to get His people into Egypt. It was in Egypt where they would grow into a great nation and it would be out of Egypt that He would deliver them in power and shape them into a holy nation that would worship and serve Him.

It is my conviction that God is trying to get His Church into Egypt, while He tries to get Egypt out of the Church. We spend all our Sundays complaining about the world around us, instead of preparing God's Josephs to go into Egypt to be deliverers.

Without revealing his identity, Joseph questioned his brothers about their family. In this way he learned for sure that Benjamin was still at home with their father. Then, accusing them of being spies, he threw them in jail. After three days, Joseph released them and insisted that they go home and return with Benjamin. As insurance, he would keep Simeon in confinement until they returned. Joseph then gave his brothers the grain they needed and sent them on their way. Unknown to them he had returned their money, hiding it in the top of their grain sacks. They discovered it on the way home.

Back in Canaan, Jacob was unwilling to let Benjamin go, fearful of losing him as he had lost Joseph. Once the food ran out again, however, and when his sons explained to him that they could not return for more grain unless Benjamin was with them, Jacob relented. Armed with a gift of nuts, honey, and spices for Joseph, and twice the amount of money as before, the brothers returned to Egypt. Benjamin was under Judah's care, who had pledged with his own life to protect him.

When Joseph saw his brothers again, and Benjamin with them, he still did not identify himself. He gave a feast for them, then loaded them up with grain for their return journey. Once again Joseph returned their money. He also ordered a servant to hide his special silver cup in Benjamin's sack, then to pursue his brothers after they left. The servant was to "discover" the "stolen" cup and make the brothers return to the city. Once this was done, and Joseph's brothers stood before him, trembling with fear, Joseph told them they could go, except for Benjamin, who would remain in Egypt as a slave.

Why did Joseph treat his brothers this way? Was it revenge, a chance to get even? No. There was no vindictiveness in Joseph's heart. He was testing his brothers. He wanted to see if over the years their character had changed. It had. Judah immediately interceded on Benjamin's behalf, offering to be Joseph's slave instead. By their actions, Joseph knew his brothers had changed. It was then that he revealed himself to them.

Then Joseph said to his brothers, "I am Joseph; does my father still live?" But his brothers could not answer him, for they were dismayed in his presence. And Joseph said to his brothers, "Please come near to me." So they came near. Then he said: "I am Joseph your brother, whom you sold into Egypt. But now, do not therefore be grieved or angry with yourselves because you sold me here; for God sent me before you to preserve life. For these two years the famine has been in the land, and there are still five years in which there will be neither plow-ing nor harvesting. And God sent me before you to preserve a posteri-ty for you in the earth, and to save your lives by a great deliverance. So now it was not you who sent me here, but God" (Genesis 45:3-8a).

Joseph was alone with his brothers when he revealed himself to them. He kissed them and embraced them, and they enjoyed a tearful, happy reunion which none of them had expected. Joseph had his broth-ers back. Through forgiveness and reconciliation they were now broth-ers in spirit as well as in flesh.

If we are going to be used by God to deliver our brothers, forgive-ness is crucial. Unforgiveness in the Church today among denomina-tions, leaders, and church members is holding back God's great plan for revival to our churches, our cities, and even our nation.

The Circle Complete

With Pharaoh's blessing, Joseph sent his brothers home with instructions to bring their father and all the rest of the family to live in Egypt. Pharaoh even provided wagons and provisions for the trip. The entire company that journeyed from Canaan numbered 70 people.

Jacob, who had mourned for Joseph ever since he disappeared, received a double blessing. He learned that his favorite son was still alive, and he received assurance of the Lord's presence with him. On the way to Egypt Jacob stopped at Beersheba and offered a sacrifice to God. There the Lord said, "I am God, the God of your father...Do not be afraid to go down to Egypt, for I will make you into a great nation there. I will go down to Egypt with you, and I will surely bring you back again. And Joseph's own hand will close your eyes" (Gen. 46:3-4 NIV). Isn't that a wonderful promise? God would always be with him, and the very son that Jacob never expected to see again would be at his bedside when he died.

Joseph was God's man for his place and time. Because of his faith-fulness a family was restored, whole nations of people were preserved during a time of famine, and the infant nation of Israel was positioned to grow and prosper. As a "savior" in his day he is a spiritual "type" of Christ.

In our own day God is raising up within His endtime Church a new generation of believers, a "Joseph generation" who, like their namesake, will be committed to "seeking their brothers"; to regaining, restoring, and preserving people, cities, and nations through the providence and power of God. Also, like Joseph, this generation will be identified by the same characteristics. Joseph was a *dreamer* who was *born at the right time*. He was a *righteous* man who was *familiar with adversity*. He was *spiritually alert* and enjoyed the *favor of God and men*.

What does it mean to be a member of the "Joseph generation"?

Chapter Five

The Joseph Generation

But you are a chosen generation, a royal priesthood, a holy nation, His own special people, that you may proclaim the praises of Him who called you out of darkness into His marvelous light; who once were not a people but are now the people of God, who had not obtained mercy but now have obtained mercy (1 Peter 2:9-10).

I believe that the Christian Church, particularly in America, is at a crossroads. As we enter a new century and millennium the challenges of "seeking our brothers" and reaching the lost with the gospel are greater than ever before. Attitudes, methods, and programs of the past are no longer adequate. New challenges call for new approaches. The lost, the needy, the hurting, and the dying—"the ones nobody wants"— are outpacing the Church's ability to keep up. We can no longer be satisfied to "do church" or to "do ministry" in the old way. We can no longer afford simply to sit inside the four walls of our church buildings and hope that the hurting come to us. Jesus commanded us to *go*.

God has always raised up in every generation a company of people strategically placed in church and society through whom He can fulfill His purpose and bring His will to pass in the earth. Joseph was such a person for his day. We have already seen how God positioned and prepared Joseph for a specific purpose. Joseph recognized the hand of God on his life. He explained to his brothers, "But as for you, you meant evil against me; *but God meant it for good,* in order to bring it about as it is this day, *to save many people alive*" (Gen. 50:20, emphasis added).

Our generation is no different. The Lord is raising up and calling out a "Joseph company"—believers who will not be content to do things the old way but, under the leadership of the Spirit, seek a fresh approach and redefine the Church for a new day and age. Fueled by passion for Christ demonstrated in compassionate ministry to others, this "Joseph generation" will be positioned to prepare the Church to reach the masses, particularly in the cities, and help bring in a great endtime harvest of souls. Like their namesake, those of the "Joseph generation" are being called out at a specific time for a specific purpose. And, like Joseph, they will reveal certain characteristics that will define their lives and experiences.

A COMPANY OF DREAMERS

And it shall come to pass afterward that I will pour out My Spirit on all flesh; your sons and your daughters shall prophesy, your old men shall dream dreams, your young men shall see visions (Joel 2:28).

Joseph was a dreamer. Not only did he manifest the ability to receive and interpret prophetic dreams, but also was able to look beyond his own circumstances and discern the activity and greater purpose of God. He was a man of vision.

In the same way, the "Joseph generation" is a company of dreamers. Not content simply to accept things as they are, they see beyond to the way God wants things to be. They are willing to step out and take risks in order to obey God's call.

Dreamers do not focus on meager human resources, but on God's infinite supply. Instead of seeing only "five loaves and two fish" they see food enough to fill five thousand stomachs with 12 basketfuls of leftovers. Rather than backing down from obstacles and opposition as "impossible" mountains to climb, dreamers know that "all things are possible to him who believes" (Mk. 9:23b). They have latched onto the truth that God "is able to do exceedingly abundantly above all that we ask or think, according to the power that works in us" (Eph. 3:20). Going beyond merely trusting God, dreamers dare to *expect* God to do great and mighty things.

Ever since God said to me, "If you'll take care of the ones nobody wants, I'll give you the ones everybody's after," we at Rock City Church have lived as dreamers. As we have set out in faith to care for the "throwaways," as we have busied ourselves in "seeking our brothers," God has blessed us, provided for us, and opened every possible door for us all over the city of Baltimore and beyond. Even as dreamers we had little idea as we began our ministries of the Hiding Place, the Nehemiah House, A Can Can Make a Difference, Adopt-A-Block, and others, of the great favor God would bestow or the magnitude of the work He would do and the lives He would change through us.

We have learned as a way of church life to dream and regularly step into God's arena to watch Him do the "impossible" in our midst. Passing through the veils of doubt and difficulty, we step into places where no one else goes and take care of people no one else wants. In the process we learn through experience that God indeed is able to do "exceedingly abundantly above all that we ask or think." The Lord has taught us that we can dream the greatest dreams for our church, our city, and our world and in Him watch those dreams become reality.

The "Joseph generation" is a company of dreamers whose dreams are limited only by their ability to believe in a God of infinite possibilities.

BORN AT THE RIGHT TIME

To everything there is a season, a time for every purpose under heaven: a time to be born...(Ecclesiastes 3:1-2a).

Nothing happens by accident in the Kingdom of Heaven. God is never taken by surprise. If there is anything that the Bible makes clear, it is that all of history is unfolding according to God's pre-ordained plan. He is the Sovereign Lord of the universe and He is in control. No matter who opposes Him, no matter how hard godless people try to thwart Him, no matter how unresponsive or disobedient His own people are, in the end God will establish all things according to His own purpose.

None of us are accidents of birth. God has always raised up at the right time the people He would use to bring about His purpose. He called Abram (Abraham) when He was ready to establish His covenant in preparation for building a nation holy to Himself. He raised up Joseph to preserve that infant nation—Jacob and his sons—so that they could increase to a great multitude in Egypt. When it was time to deliver that multitude from Egyptian bondage, God protected, prepared, and called Moses for the assignment. Centuries later, under Persian rule, the Jewish exiles were threatened with annihilation from Haman, the Persian prime minister. God raised up Esther, a lowly Jewish maiden, to be queen to the king of Persia, and thus be the deliverer of her people. Her uncle Mordecai had said to her, "Yet who knows whether you have come to the kingdom for such a time as this?" (Esther 4:14b) Finally, at the right time, Jesus came. "But when the fullness of the time had come, God sent forth His Son, born of a woman, born under the law, to redeem those who were under the law, that we might receive the adoption as sons" (Gal. 4:4-5).

Joseph was born at the end of an era and was a witness to great change. He saw the end of one "season of time"—his family's first sojourn in Canaan—and the beginning of another—the long Egyptian period. More than four centuries would pass before that season of time would end with the appearance of Moses and the exodus from Egypt.

Like Joseph of old, in our own day God is raising up the "Joseph generation," a company of believers who are born at the right time. In His sovereign will God has brought us onto the earth at this specific time for a specific reason. We too are witnesses to the end of a season of time and the beginning of another. Great changes are underway in both the Church and the world. New leadership is arising in the Church, along with new ways of doing things. There is a renewed focus on worship and the presence of God, as well as on personal intimacy with the Lord. God is pouring out His Spirit in fresh, new ways all over the world and many believers are experiencing true revival.

With renewed interest and passion for the presence of God, there's also a renewed passion to reach out to mankind. I call this the "Martha and Mary principle." Jesus visited their house in Bethany more than any other house. Why? Because both women, living in the same house, ministered to Jesus out of their passion. Mary ministered to His divinity, while Martha ministered to His humanity. If the Church can see this principle, that both can live in the same house, then every *dead brother* will come alive like Lazarus did.

The world is changing as well. Over the past decade we have witnessed breathtaking changes in the political climate across the globe. Ten years ago, how many people would have believed that before the end of the 20th century Soviet communism would be a dead issue in the world? With the fall of the Soviet Union, new avenues for the gospel have opened up in the countries that were formerly under its boot. General interest in "spirituality" is at an all-time high. People all over the world are searching desperately for truth. Most do not know where to find it. The whole earth is ripe for a visitation from God.

As with Queen Esther, the "Joseph generation" is being born now "for such a time as this." God is planting in the hearts of His people the burden and the call to be a "Joseph" for their cities and their nations. He is preparing His Church to bring in and receive the awesome spiritual harvest that is to come. There is no time like the present. What an age it is in which to be alive! We will be able to see the transition from the old to the new, and be able to celebrate God's goodness in the midst of both! Where will God take our country and the world in the next ten or twenty years? Whatever He does, it will be marvelous! "Behold, I will do a new thing, now it shall spring forth" (Is. 43:19a). The "Joseph generation," born at the right time, is part of His plan.

A RIGHTEOUS COMPANY

Then the righteous will shine forth as the sun in the kingdom of their Father (Matthew 13:43a).

God always brings forth a righteous company in the midst of unrighteousness. Joseph stood out in the crowd wherever he was because he steadfastly walked in righteousness. He refused to surrender his integrity or compromise his character, no matter what. Joseph's stand for righteousness came at a heavy price: persecution and treachery from his brothers, followed by years of slavery in Egypt, and slander by Potiphar's wife, followed by several years in an Egyptian dungeon. When the time was right, however, God elevated Joseph to a position where in his righteousness he could "shine forth as the sun in the kingdom."

The Lord has raised the "Joseph generation" to walk in righteousness that we too may "shine forth as the sun in the kingdom of [our] Father." I'm not talking about some putrid self-righteousness where we have an exalted attitude toward ourselves and think we are better than everybody else. I *am* talking about righteousness that comes from right living: living right before God and before people. True righteousness comes only from God. It is imparted to us by the grace of God through the Spirit of Christ. Our part as believers is to "work out" that righteousness in day-to-day living.

Righteous people refuse to live by the world's standards. They are scrupulously honest in their business dealings and in every other dimension of life. Committed to moral purity, they show honor and respect in every relationship. They don't lie, they don't cheat, and they don't deceive. They don't live half-baked Christian lives. They don't violate their own conscience or compromise their convictions for personal gain. Their deepest motivation is to bring honor and glory to God in everything they do and say. The "Joseph generation" will stand out as different because of their righteousness.

One night I received a call from a young man in our church who had recently been saved. "Pastor Bart, I have a problem," he said. "My partner and I have a printing business and we have been illegally using over $50,000 worth of stolen, copied materials." The Holy Spirit had brought him under deep conviction about this and he wanted to erase from their computers all of the illegal material. I told him that God would honor his act of obedience and would do something for him that would stagger him and those around him. The righteousness of Christ in him was rising up to manifest itself in his life. It is our obedience to such conviction that brings about in us the righteousness that God is after in each of our lives.

Many unbelievers level at Christians the charge of being "narrow." If by this they mean that we take a stance of "no compromise" with regard to sin and anything ungodly, then each of us should be eager to confess "guilty as charged." The way of the Lord is a narrow road. Jesus said, "Enter through the narrow gate. For wide is the gate and broad is the road that leads to destruction, and many enter through it. But small is the gate and narrow the road that leads to life, and only a few find it" (Mt. 7:13-14 NIV). The closer we walk with the Lord, the narrower the path becomes. At the same time our joy, our love, and our compassion for others grow wider and wider. It is the *way* of the Lord that is narrow, *not* His love, grace, and mercy.

The Bible says that in the last days people will become more and more deceived and will give themselves over to the "itching ear principle," wanting to hear only those things that tickle their ears and make them feel good rather than truth that can change their lives. God is raising up in the midst of this nation and in the midst of the Church a company—the "Joseph generation"—who will stand for righteousness without compromise or apology and refuse to be a part of any unrighteous causes.

FAMILIAR WITH ADVERSITY

We are hard pressed on every side, yet not crushed; we are perplexed, but not in despair; persecuted, but not forsaken; struck down, but not destroyed (2 Corinthians 4:8-9).

These days nobody likes to talk about adversity, even in church. We much prefer to talk about the blessings, the promises, and the good and positive things. How often do we hear sermons about the afflictions and hardships of godly people in the Bible? Those are the parts of the Scriptures that we would rather just skip over. Yet, adversity is an unavoidable part of life. Instead of fearing adversity we should remember that even it fits into God's plan for us. Adversity, when approached from God's perspective, builds strength, faith, and character.

The Bible clearly teaches that there is a balance between blessing and suffering. God brings famine and judgment, but He also brings mercy, grace, and hope. God both afflicts and heals, but both have a redemptive purpose. David wrote, "Before I was afflicted I went astray, but now I obey Your word....It was good for me to be afflicted so that I might learn Your decrees" (Ps. 119:67,71 NIV). There are times when God opens the heavens and times when He closes them. Both serve His purpose.

Joseph knew adversity. He was torn from his home and family, enslaved, slandered, imprisoned, and forgotten by men. God did not forget him, however. Joseph's adversity strengthened his godliness and his character, and in due time God raised him up to fulfill his destiny.

Jesus knew adversity. Hated by the religious leaders, rejected by the very people He came to save, misunderstood by His own disciples, Jesus finally was nailed to a cross to get Him out of the way. "He is despised and rejected by men, a Man of sorrows and acquainted with grief" (Is. 53:3a). The "Joseph generation" that God is raising up today is a people who, like their Master, will be familiar with adversity.

One Sunday morning in church I asked, "What would you do if God took your child? Would you stop serving Him?" If that question makes you uncomfortable, remember that sometimes life forces us to face up to uncomfortable situations.

In 1987 Rachel, our oldest child and only daughter, was diagnosed with Hodgkins disease. She was 15 at the time. In a matter of days, our lives changed drastically. Adversity was staring us in the face, big time. Rather than improving quickly as we originally hoped, the situation got progressively worse from one day to the next. From an initial possibility of affecting only one area of her neck, Rachel's cancer quickly grew to Stage 4A (4B was the worst), moving into one of her lungs as well. Over a period of 18 months we went through two major surgeries, several minor surgeries, eight months of chemotherapy, and six weeks of radiation treatments with her.

During this time Coralee and I had to face the question, "What will we do if God takes our daughter?" In the end there was only one answer. "Lord, we will love You and serve You."

Now, 13 years later, each of us can look back and see how we grew and prospered, how our character was built and strengthened, and how God accomplished in and through us what could not have been done otherwise. Through it all, God had his hand on Rachel. She was then and is now a living testimony to God's mercy, grace, and power. Today Rachel is cancer free, married, and has a son. That with which the enemy sought to destroy us God used to build and strengthen us. He used Rachel's illness to focus her life on her professional calling to work with children who are terminally ill.

God brings, or at least allows, adversity to come into our lives in order to teach us how to deal with it. Trials and testing are inescapable in life, so we must learn how to handle them in a victorious and God-honoring way. Through adversity God also proves us to reveal what is really in our hearts. He wants to build in us the same posture and attitude as that of Job when he said, "The Lord gave, and the Lord has taken away; blessed be the name of the Lord" (Job 1:21b), and "Though He slay me, yet will I trust Him" (Job 13:15a).

If we are part of the "Joseph generation," our commitment to the Lord must be more than a fair-weather faith that disappears at the first sign of trouble. Adversity, when faced through the power of the Spirit, is a faith-builder. The apostle Peter, reminding his readers that their salvation was secure through God's power, then wrote,

In this you greatly rejoice, though now for a little while, if need be, you have been grieved by various trials, that the genuineness of your faith, being much more precious than gold that perishes, though it is tested by fire, may be found to praise, honor, and glory at the revelation of Jesus Christ, whom having not seen you love (1 Peter 1:6-8a).

Adversity comes upon everyone in the world. Why should we expect to be exempt simply because we are believers? In our case, adversity from God is a sign both of His love for us and of our relationship with Him as His children. "The Lord disciplines those He loves, and He punishes everyone He accepts as a son. Endure hardship as discipline; God is treating you as sons. For what son is not disciplined by his father?" (Heb. 12:6-7 NIV) As God's children, the "Joseph generation" will experience His discipline. They will be familiar with adversity.

A Spiritually Alert Company

Be self-controlled and alert. Your enemy the devil prowls around like a roaring lion looking for someone to devour (1 Peter 5:8 NIV).

One of the secrets of Joseph's success was that he was spiritually alert. Even from a young age he apparently was aware of God's hand on his life. He may not have known always where that hand was leading him or exactly how everything would play out in the end, but he was confident that God was in control. It was Joseph's spiritual alertness that enabled him to maintain his integrity under every circumstance.

Eventually, Joseph's integrity and spiritual alertness got him out of prison and into the position of prime minister to Pharaoh. Have you ever wondered why Joseph didn't simply go home at that point? He was no longer a slave or a prisoner; he was a free man. Why didn't he return to Canaan to see his father and family? Joseph was alert enough to recognize the unique and particular call of God on his life. He knew that God had placed him where he was for a purpose. He knew also that he was responsible to God for fulfilling that purpose. As Joseph remained faithful to God's call, God eventually brought Joseph's family to *him*. When we take care of the things that are important to God, He will take care of the things that are important to us.

Being spiritually alert means being awake to the reality that living for God is not confined by the "religious" status quo. The Lord is raising up a "Joseph generation" of spiritually alert people who will no longer blandly and blindly accept the religious "norms" of the day. Many congregations have fallen asleep in the midst of their forms and their rituals and their traditions. They are like the men Paul described, who have a form of godliness but deny its power (see 2 Tim. 3:5). In this state they are in serious danger of missing God's great visitation to His people in our generation.

When was the last time you slept through your alarm in the morning? It buzzed or beeped or clanged, and through a fog of half-sleep you shut it off and promptly zonked out again. An hour later you suddenly woke up with a start. Realizing you were late, you scrambled around frantically trying to pull things together. Your whole day was thrown off-kilter.

It's important to be awake and alert in order to be prepared for what life throws at us. That is one reason Jesus' disciples failed Him on the night He was arrested. Jesus had entered the Garden of Gethsemane to pray, asking His friends to "Stay here and watch with Me" (Mt. 26:38b). Instead, they fell asleep. In disappointment Jesus asked them, "Could you not watch with Me one hour?" (Mt. 26:40b) When the crisis came, Jesus was ready. His disciples were not. Wakened suddenly from their slumber and caught unprepared, they fled in fear and confusion.

Today God is trying to rouse His people. He has set off an alarm to wake the nations, but many in the West, including America, are sleeping right through it. Because so many American churches are asleep, American cities are asleep, unaware of approaching disaster. The Jerusalem of Jesus' day was in this condition and our Lord wept over the city.

If you had known, even you, especially in this your day, the things that make for your peace! But now they are hidden from your eyes. For days will come upon you when your enemies will build an embankment around you, surround you and close you in on every side, and level you, and your children within you, to the ground; and they will not leave in you one stone upon another, because you did not know the time of your visitation (Luke 19:42-44).

God's heart is to rescue our cities and our nation. He is calling us to wake up and stay alert. Some, however, just want to sleep, content and comfortable in their religious routine. There are others who are responding to God's alarm. They are rising up and paying attention, listening to the voice of their Lord. A new spiritual sensitivity has awakened in their inner being, causing them to cry out, "Lord, I don't want to sleep through my day of visitation. I don't want to miss out on Your purpose for my life. I want to carry out everything You have placed me here on earth to do." The "Joseph generation" is like that.

IN FAVOR WITH GOD AND MAN

Let not mercy and truth forsake you; bind them around your neck, write them on the tablet of your heart, and so find favor and high esteem in the sight of God and man (Proverbs 3:3-4).

How do we find favor with God and man? We must embrace mercy and truth; bind them around our necks and write them on our hearts. Here again is the reunion of "Mary and Martha," of passion and compassion. Mercy represents the compassion we extend to others in Christ's name. Truth represents passion: our passionate devotion to Christ, who is the truth, as we walk the "narrow way" with Him. These two linked in unity will bring "favor and high esteem" with both God and men.

Most people like to be around those who have prospered in the Lord. Even if they don't know God, they like to get close to someone who has been blessed, hoping that some of it will spill over onto them. Whether or not they know it or admit it, people are hungry for a touch from God.

The "Joseph generation" is a company upon whom God's favor rests. Like trees planted by streams of water they yield fruit in their season, their leaf does not wither, and they prosper in everything they do (see Ps. 1:3). This does not mean prospering financially, although that may occur as well. God's prosperity is primarily spiritual in nature. When His favor rests on us, we prosper as He brings about in and through our lives circumstances, outcomes, and events in accordance with His will that we could never achieve for ourselves. When people witness God doing through us things that only He can do, He receives the glory and they are drawn to Him.

Amazing things begin to happen whenever God sets His favor on us. At Rock City Church we have ample testimony to this. For example, we go regularly into the Baltimore prison system to minister. Every door is open to us. We enjoy the favor of city leaders as well as penal system and law enforcement officials. Not just anyone is allowed to come in and do what we do.

Some years ago a young woman in our church told me her story. She had been an inmate during a time that we had ministered at the prison, and had been touched by the Lord while we were there. A short time later, when she went to court to answer charges against her, the clerk of the court pulled her aside. He said to her, "We don't understand it, but we can't find a single record on you. We don't even know who you are. So, all we can tell you is to go home."

She didn't have to hear *that* twice! She went home, and from there went to church. She remembered how God had met her in that prison cell and she pursued Him once she got out. She saw the favor of God on her life.

On another occasion a man representing a major American power tool manufacturer appeared out of the blue in my driveway. He was a complete stranger to me. Almost before I knew what happened, he had given our church a bunch of giant, brand-new industrial tools for us to use in construction! (We were building a new sanctuary.)

God gives His people favor! These are only three examples of the kinds of things we have seen God do over and over through the years. Even more amazing, however, is the favor God has shown toward us in the area of our social ministries. These have grown and prospered far beyond what any of us expected or even dreamed at the beginning. The Hiding Place, the Nehemiah House, A Can Can Make a Difference, and Adopt-A-Block are ministries that the Lord has greatly blessed and is using to help our church reach the city of Baltimore.

Chapter Six

Healing the Hurting

For He will hide me in His shelter in the day of trouble (Psalm 27:5a NRSV).

One day in 1985 I was picketing a Baltimore abortion clinic along with a number of other people. At one point a young, pregnant African-American girl approached me, holding up her pink Planned Parenthood slip. She then tore up the slip and threw the pieces at me, saying rather defiantly, "Okay, Preacher, *now* what are you going to do?"

I didn't know how to respond. I had nothing to say because there was nothing I *could* do for her. At that moment the Lord convicted me deeply in my heart. I realized that standing there with a protest sign in my hand did nothing for her. That very day I put away my placard. I had picketed for the last time. Instead, I set out to *do* something for the *tomorrows* of this girl and others like her, and for their babies.

Rock City Church is located on the top of a hill in the northwestern suburbs of Baltimore. The site of our original sanctuary was separated from an adjacent hill by a deep ravine. Often I found myself standing on our hill looking out over the other hill and seeing it as ours. Like Caleb of old, I wanted my mountain (see Josh. 14:1-14). The only problem was that this "mountain," like Caleb's, was already occupied.

Three houses dotted the adjacent hilltop. The total property area was about 24 acres. One day I went over and walked the property, declaring as I did so, "This land is ours! We are going to own this land!" Some folks in the church protested, "But Pastor Bart, people *live* in those houses, and now you're walking around claiming their property!" All I could say was, "This land is going to be ours!" I knew that somehow God would bring it to pass. Sure enough, all three homeowners eventually came to us and sold us their property.

The first house that became available to us was the one closest to our property. Situated on eight acres, the large, brick colonial-style house had been built in the 1920s. One day Coralee and I went with the real estate agent to see the house. As I stood on the front porch I felt God say to me, "You'll call it the Hiding Place." I immediately tried to remember the appropriate Scripture verse. "You are my hiding place; You shall preserve me from trouble; You shall surround me with songs of deliverance" (Ps. 32:7). I barely had time to whisper to Coralee what the Lord had said before the owner of the house ushered us inside.

He invited us to sit down and then said, "Well, Reverend, what are you going to do for me?"

"What kind of deal can you give me?" I asked. Then I added, "I want you to give me the house."

For a few moments I thought he was going to swallow the stubby cigar he had in his mouth. His wife quickly came to his rescue. "Reverend," she said to me, "let me take you upstairs to see the rest of the house."

Leading us into one of the upstairs bedrooms, she walked over to the bed, got up on her tiptoes, and slid off a piece of wood from the paneled wall above it. "This is where my father put all of the jewelry and other valuables before going on vacation. He didn't like to use banks, so he stored everything in this secret compartment. We call it 'the hiding place.' "

What confirmation! I knew God was in this! My excitement grew as we toured the rest of the house. There was no doubt in my mind that we were going to buy it. Before we left, Coralee said to the real estate agent, "You won't sell this house; you won't even show it to another person.

God has said that it's our house." I told Coralee later, "That's not how you influence real estate people."

A year went by and, sure enough, no one else had even looked at the house, much less bought it. So, it became the property of Rock City Church—at $100,000 less than the original asking price. Some time later we were able to buy the second house on that hill, and then the third one. Finally, the entire hill belonged to us. God had taken our dream and done something supernatural. We had our "mountain."

A Refuge in the Storm

The Hiding Place opened in 1986 as a place of refuge for women in crisis situations. Most are young, unmarried, and pregnant. Some are addicted to drugs or alcohol. Many harbor deep hurt and anger, particularly toward men. All are at a place in life where they have nowhere to turn. Abandoned and often abused by their boyfriends (or husbands, fathers, grandfathers, brothers, etc.), or rejected by their families, these young women enter the Hiding Place with little understanding of a stable family environment. Quite often they have no clue either of how to care for the baby they will soon give birth to, or of how to live as godly women. The Hiding Place exists to address all of these needs.

The Hiding Place is a seven-bed residential facility where women in crisis receive love, care, and encouragement in a healthy, Christian family environment, with the emphasis on *Christian* and *family*. It provides a home for many who have never had a real home. Women who enter the program are established in a home structure with a daily routine of work and recreation. All residents take part in the normal domestic chores and activities necessary for keeping house: washing dishes, doing laundry, mopping floors, etc. They learn how to plan and prepare meals, and mealtimes are opportunities for fellowship, questions, discussion, and sharing. The directors of the home, who live at the facility with their family, take part in the everyday life and activity of the home, right along with the residents. It truly is a *family* environment.

Providing a strong Christian atmosphere at the Hiding Place is the highest priority. The only sure and certain answer to the life problems of these women is found in Christ, and they are surrounded with opportunities to know Him and follow Him. Organized Bible study is part of the daily routine of the women. They also have regular opportunities to attend church and participate in church-related activities. Through this environment of Christian love and emphasis on spiritual truth, most of the women who come to the Hiding Place discover during their stay the transforming power of Christ in their lives.

The Hiding Place is not simply a shelter for women in need. It is a fully organized program designed to minister to the physical, emotional, and spiritual needs of the residents. Each woman who enters the program has a wide range of services available to her, including:

- Advocacy—A support person or family is assigned to every woman at the Hiding Place, to befriend, encourage, and assist her during her stay. A pregnant woman in the program is assigned a specially trained helper who will accompany her to the hospital at the time of delivery and remain with her until after the baby is born.

- Homemaking—Each resident receives training in basic domestic skills through participation in household chores and in meal planning and preparation.

- Recreation—Leisure time is important for developing the whole person, so regular "fun" activities are planned, such as family outings, shopping trips, sporting events, handcrafts, and hobbies.

- Medical—Local physicians and nurses volunteer their services to provide medical care for the house residents. Expectant mothers receive both prenatal and postnatal care.

- Education—Each woman is encouraged to continue her education during her stay. Tutoring and guidance in academic matters are provided for this purpose.

- Counseling—Residents of the program receive assistance in discovering how best to develop their individual gifts, talents, and abilities in order to provide for a successful future.

In addition, the program at the Hiding Place includes "Buds to Roses," a nine-month Christ-centered Life Skills curriculum that was developed to help nurture, encourage, and build up women in crisis and give them the natural and spiritual tools they need to reach their full potential in life. Divided into three "trimesters," this program begins with basic and fundamental issues such as self-image and domestic skills, and advances the women to progressively higher levels of confidence, ability, and maturity. At the heart of "Buds to Roses" is the Life Plan, drawn up during the first trimester, in which each woman describes her personal aspirations and dreams and develops a clear and specific plan for attaining her goals. The entire "Buds to Roses" curriculum is designed to help them achieve their goals and realize their dreams.

Since its beginning almost 15 years ago, the Hiding Place has seen over five hundred girls and young women come through its doors. Some were as young as 14 years old. Over 350 babies have been born to the house. It is truly a "refuge in the storm," where women who have been battered by life can find a safe harbor in which to mend their sails, reorient their compass, get their lives together, and chart a new course with Christ as their Pilot. The stories that follow are true testimonies of women whose lives were touched and changed forever by the love and grace of God through the ministry of the Hiding Place.

SARAH NIELSON

Born into a dysfunctional family, to an alcoholic father and drug addicted mother, Sarah Nielson grew up in an environment of abuse and confusion. She was forced to leave home when she was 15, and at 18 suffered a nervous breakdown. After spending some time in a mental hospital in Philadelphia, it seemed she was about to get her life together. Sarah met and married a man who was a recovering alcoholic. She also enrolled in a computer programming training school. Her husband quickly began to resent the long hours she spent studying. After only eight months of marriage and only six weeks before Sarah graduated, he left her for another woman.

Devastated and vulnerable, Sarah was taken advantage of by another man who had a record of domestic abuse and who, against her will, moved into her apartment with her. Soon after this, Sarah discovered that she was pregnant. When she refused her boyfriend's demand to get an abortion, he tried to kill her.

"I was lying on the floor," Sarah recalls, "and his hands were around my neck. He was trying to suffocate me. I was lying flat on the floor and something just picked me up and stood me right on my feet. I never even bent my knees or anything. I felt like it was an angel that picked me up and spared my life, because he could have killed me. I had bruises on my neck from where he tried to suffocate me.

"I went to the Domestic Violence Center in Westchester [Pennsylvania] and I was protected from him there while they processed his case in the court system. I met a social worker and she told me about the Hiding Place."

Sarah stayed with the social worker until an opening became available at the Hiding Place. She was unable to get into her house without her boyfriend trying to bother her, so the police let her in just long enough to grab a few essentials. Everything else she left behind: furniture, clothes, books—all her possessions. When Sarah moved to Baltimore and the Hiding Place, she made a clean break with her past. "It was a totally new beginning," she says.

Sarah was already a Christian when she came to the Hiding Place, but was very immature in her faith. "I was saved when I was 15 years old. I asked the Lord into my life but I never walked with Him. I never went to church. I started going to church for the first time at the Rock City Church. I had never felt the presence of God before until I came to Rock City Church, and it was just so powerful; I had never experienced anything like that before.

"I had some really incredible encounters with the Lord while I was at the Hiding Place. I was very introverted and shut myself away in my room and studied my Bible. I didn't know how to relate to anybody because I had never really developed any social skills. I could barely express myself. I didn't really know who I was; I didn't really have an identity. I was just kind of existing. For the first time in my life, at Rock City Church I started figuring out what makes me laugh, what makes me cry, how I feel about certain things, my opinions—what makes me a person. I never really knew that before. Because of the abuse I was in at home I had no chance to discover who I was. For the first time I was getting to know myself and to know the Lord."

When her baby was born, Sarah gave him up for adoption. She knew at the time that she was not emotionally ready to raise a child. Her son was adopted into a Christian family in Virginia Beach, Virginia.

Two years after coming to the Hiding Place, Sarah met Dave, her future husband. They dated for awhile, and even attended marriage classes, but then broke up. Five years later they got together again and, since they both were more ready emotionally, they married.

Life has changed dramatically for Sarah since she first came to Baltimore. "We have a new house; we have two cars; we have a sweet little puppy. Our lives have been so blessed. God has just provided for all our needs since we've been at Rock City Church."

Sarah Nielson is one example of how a broken, battered, confused, and hurting person can be healed and brought into victory through the grace, mercy, and power of God. The Hiding Place provided an environment through which God met Sarah, healed her, and set her life on the right track.

STACEY GRAY

When Stacey Gray arrived at the Hiding Place, she was nine months pregnant with her second child. Her first, a daughter, was in foster care. Stacey's daughter had been removed from her custody because she had abused the child. As with many abusive parents, Stacey herself was a victim of abuse. Her parents were evicted from their apartment when she was 17. With nowhere else to go, Stacey and her younger brother went to live with some family friends. The arrangement seemed to work for awhile, but then for some reason turned abusive. Stacey's guardians took her food stamps and began beating her. She often had bruises on her body, a black eye or a bloody nose.

During this highly destructive and unstable time in her life, Stacey found herself pregnant. She had no idea of the kinds of demands that a baby would make on her and no clue on how to raise a child. Consequently, at the age of nine months her baby was placed in foster care.

Not long after this, Stacey was pregnant again, but by a different man. She was still in the same abusive home situation, but was tired of being beaten and taken advantage of. Late in her pregnancy Stacey heard about the Hiding Place from a social worker she had met during the case involving her first child. Since it meant a safe haven from abuse, Stacey decided to go there. After returning home under a protective police escort, Stacey gathered her belongings and moved to the Hiding Place. Because of the strong and distinctive Christian atmosphere of the house, Stacey gave her heart and life to Christ shortly after her arrival.

She was baptized at Rock City Church and gave birth to her second daughter two days later.

Stacey's second baby was placed with the same foster family who was caring for her first daughter. This fine Christian family has since formally adopted both girls. At the time Stacey came to the Hiding Place, she couldn't take care of herself, much less a baby. During her three years at the Hiding Place, Stacey grew in her faith and learned how to care for herself. Now graduated from the Hiding Place, Stacey is currently participating in the Extended Family Program, which is designed to help women transition from the Hiding Place to living on their own. In this program, Stacey lives with a loving extended family to give her the chance to learn how to live alone without being alone and to apply what she learned at the Hiding Place. Eventually, she will transition into her own home.

Today, Stacey Gray has a successful job as a waitress. Her excellent service and warm, ready smile have made her popular with the restaurant's regular customers, many of whom ask specifically for her when they visit. She sees her two daughters regularly every month, and the girls look forward to spending time with the woman they know as "Mommy Stacey."

TRACI STRAWBRIDGE

"God has just totally, totally turned my life around 100 percent" says Traci Strawbridge. "If it wasn't for Pastor Bart, the one who offers all of this, I wouldn't be where I am today. If it wasn't for his people being obedient to the Lord and going under his direction, I would be dead or dying from AIDS or something. I don't know why God picked me, but thank You, Jesus! I know so many people who could have this. I don't understand it, but God picked me."

The Lord has completely delivered Traci from a life of drugs and alcohol, and the Hiding Place was a key factor in her deliverance.

By the time Traci was a teenager, her life was already in turmoil. Her parents divorced, and by the time she was in her mid-to-late teens, both of them were in their third marriages. Traci began smoking pot when she was 13 and got involved in shoplifting. She ended up in court several times.

When Traci was 15, her mother sent her to Germany to live with her brother's girlfriend, in hopes that Traci would "grow up." Instead, because Germany had no minimum drinking age, Traci spent a lot of time in the bars, drinking and getting high on drugs, which were easy to get in Germany. The girlfriend kicked Traci out after a year, complaining that she was partying too much.

Traci returned to her mother, but ran away a lot because she didn't want to be there. Finally, she tried living with her father and his third wife. Traci tried to hide her drinking and drugs from her father, but he was a policeman and could detect the signs. His wife gave him a choice: either her or Traci. Traci moved out and her father basically gave up on her because she was so uncontrollable. They didn't see or speak to each other for years.

Sixteen now, Traci moved in with a stripper and her boyfriend, and soon began snorting crank. By this time she was living to get high. Sometimes she would stay high for a week at a time snorting crank. When Traci was 17 she enrolled in beautician's school. While in school, she began to smoke crack. Despite her addictions and being high most of the time, she became an excellent hairdresser, in demand by many customers who regularly requested her to do their hair.

Completely on her own now, Traci went from house to house and man to man, smoking crack, getting drunk, and living a wild lifestyle. Then, over a short period of time, both her best friend and her boyfriend died. A few years later another friend—the man who had helped Traci get through beautician school, and had always been available for her—died. This drove Traci even deeper into smoking crack. Her life really began to fall apart. Up until then she had somehow kept everything together. Now she was losing jobs and her credit was suffering.

Traci realized that she had a serious problem with drugs and alcohol. She was also a heavy smoker—two to five packs a day. In her heart she wanted to quit, and tried. She returned home to her mother. She went to AA meetings, got sponsors to support and encourage her, and even went into rehab more than once. She tried counselors and psychiatrists. Nothing worked. She simply could not kick her habits. No matter what she did or how hard she tried, Traci could not get clean. Her addictions were too strong.

One day a man named Lou, who was a member of Rock City Church, was in Traci's chair as she did his hair. At the time, Traci was enrolled in an outpatient rehab program, still trying to get clean. Lou began telling her about his life as a drug addict, how he had tried to quit, had been in rehab, and nothing had worked. Then he told her how Christ had set him free and how different his life was now. Traci didn't say much, but she listened. Lou's life sounded just like hers.

Even though Traci did not believe in God at that time in her life, she told Lou that she would come to his church and "check it out." That night Traci came to Rock City Church. Kingsley Fletcher and Tommy Tenney were there. Lou and his wife sat with Traci. At first Traci thought she was in the wrong place. Everyone around her seemed "wacky" with their arms raised and people lying on the floor. When Lou's wife led Traci toward the front, Traci warned her, "I'm *not* falling on that floor!"

Traci remembers what happened next. "Kingsley Fletcher put his hand on my head and said, 'God is healing you right now of your alcohol addiction.' He began praying over me. Instantly tears started rolling down my face, and I was out. I was on the floor. I was instantly healed. I just couldn't believe it. I knew absolutely, beyond a shadow of a doubt that there was a God who had healed me *instantly* in a prayer. After spending thousands and thousands of dollars of the state's money, I couldn't get clean, and God did it just like that."

For the next six months Traci was very faithful in church and seemed to be completely clean and free of her addictions. Then, because she wasn't "pressed in" to God enough, she backslid and fell right back into her old practices. She was drinking and getting high again, and this time was worse than before. Traci had absolutely no control over it.

After spending a month in jail for assault, Traci was back on the street, where she immediately got high again and stayed that way for a week or more. When she finally realized that she could not handle what was happening in her life anymore, she called the Hiding Place. Traci had heard of it before, and some in the church had encouraged her to go there, but she had refused because she didn't want to give up her freedom. Now she was ready to do whatever it took to get clean and stay that way.

The first few weeks at the Hiding Place were rough for Traci, as she had to discover who she was and learn how to deal with life and with her feelings without the "cover" of being high. As the days went by, she began to change. Traci got clean again in the Hiding Place, this time for good. She credits the discipline, the daily routine, and, most of all, the *unconditional love* at the Hiding Place for making the difference in her life. Also, the regular worship at Rock City Church helped her make it week by week.

"My life is completely changed. I do not think the same way I thought before. I'm out on my own now, and it's awesome. You know what the most awesome part is? I have all the freedom I want. I can do anything I want to do and nobody's going to know about it. I have no desire whatsoever—and it's not even hard not to have that desire—I just have no desire to get high, I have no desire to smoke a cigarette, I have no desire to cuss. I don't even want to watch television. I have become so disciplined. God has just totally renewed my mind, and it was all through the Word. I couldn't even feel the change, but now that I look back, the Bible has totally renewed my mind completely."

Today Traci works in the office at Rock City Church, is growing in her faith, and remains very active and involved in the ministry of the church. She has reconciled with her father, who is still a policeman, and they have become best of friends. He has even become her coach in competitive bicycling. Traci has her eyes set on a state bicycling championship, so she can give all the glory to God.

Sarah Niclson, Stacey Gray, and Traci Strawbridge are only three of the hundreds of young women whose lives have been transformed by the love of God through the ministry of the Hiding Place. For all of them, the home is a literal fulfillment of the words from the 27th Psalm: "For He will hide me in His shelter in the day of trouble" (Ps. 27:5a NRSV).

Chapter Seven

Harboring the Homeless

Is it not to share your bread with the hungry, and bring the homeless poor into your house; when you see the naked, to cover them, and not to hide yourself from your own kin? (Isaiah 58:7 NRSV)

One of the ways God has richly blessed our ministries of compassion at Rock City Church is the favor He has given us in the secular community. Much of our support comes from our church members and from other churches and Christian organizations. The truly amazing thing, however, is the strong cooperation, sponsorship, and financial support we receive from city and county officials, government agencies, law enforcement bodies, health care providers, commercial businesses, private foundations, and individuals. One of the best examples of this is Nehemiah House, our shelter for homeless men.

Nehemiah House really had its beginning in the late 1980s when we opened a small shelter for men. This was not obedience to some "thus sayeth the Lord" command, but simply a response to an existing need. God *had* charged us to "take care of the ones nobody wants," and as we set out to do so, they came. Homeless men showed up, needing help and a place to stay. Operating such a shelter was almost second nature to me. I had run a halfway house for men in the mid 1970s and, because of my background, I could relate well to them. During my wild dope and surfing days, drug addicts and homeless men had been some of my best friends.

Initially, our youth pastor was in charge of the shelter. The house itself, which belonged to a man in the church, needed a lot of work. It looked as though it had been bombed out. There were areas on the second floor where we couldn't allow an oversized person to walk, for fear that he might fall through. It was a place to start, however, and was good enough for a bunch of guys who desperately needed somewhere to get off the street, be delivered from their drug or alcohol addiction, and get their lives right with God. It wasn't long before God began to open up this ministry in amazing ways.

DOES THIS REALLY WORK?

One day a local Christian businessman asked me to help him with a vision that he had for assisting battered women. At the time, he was working with the county to purchase a piece of property to build transitional housing for these women. At his request I accompanied him to a meeting with a county official to discuss his plan. I went as a favor to him and to provide moral support; I had no official status in the meeting. God had other ideas.

As the two men talked, the county official suddenly stood up and said in frustration, "I'm tired of working with you. You've dragged your feet long enough." I sat there thinking, *Lord, what am I doing here? This is not where I want to be.* The county official went on. "Do you know what I need? I need a shelter for men."

Since I had just opened one, I spoke up. "Well, I just opened one." He looked at me for a moment, then instructed his secretary to make an appointment with me. Turning back to me he asked, "Will you come see me?" I don't know whatever became of the home for battered women, but a couple of days later I was back in his office to discuss a homeless shelter.

His first words to me were, "Reverend, can you do it?" I replied, "Yes, I think so." Then he asked, "Does this really work? Do people's lives really change? Do they really get off drugs?" We talked a little longer and he asked me to return with some specific information. He was not a Christian and was looking for evidence of real people who had kicked drugs or alcohol and who had gotten their lives cleaned up.

Two weeks later I returned to his office, bringing with me a man from our church who was a professional builder. We laid open before him a whole portfolio full of pictures and testimonies of some of the "regular people" in our church who had been released from bondage to drugs, alcohol, prostitution, stealing, and other things. They weren't hard to find. They were serving as my assistant pastors, church leaders, secretaries, janitors—you name it. I did not include my own picture or story, for fear of completely blowing him away!

The county official examined the portfolio, then looked at me. With amazement in his voice he asked as he had two weeks before, "Do you really think you can do this? Does this really work? I've never met anyone who has truly been delivered from this kind of lifestyle of drugs and crime." So, I told him *my* story. As I related my tale of anger, drugs, jail, being shot at, and how Christ had saved me from it all, his eyes got bigger and bigger. Just as I was beginning to wonder if I'd made a huge mistake he said, "How much money do you need to build this shelter?"

The building contractor who was with me gave a figure of $300,000. "That's no problem," the official replied. "Money is not an issue; homelessness is. It's growing every day and we've got to do something about it." By this time I was really getting excited about this meeting! We left his office with a definitive plan to build a shelter for homeless men.

When the time came for us to receive the money, the county official called me. "We may have a problem," he said. I thought, *Oh boy, here's the catch.* "The check was written for $351,000 instead of $300,000. Is that a problem?" I assured him *very* quickly that it was *no* problem at all!

That was in 1991. Since then, we have built three times. The original, old, "bombed out" house is where the men in Phase Three (transitional phase) now live, and today it is as nice a place as you could find. Over the years we have received from Baltimore County, including operational funds, more than 1.7 million dollars for Nehemiah House.

Until this year, the shelter housed 31 men (including four in Phase Three transition), serving over 22,000 meals a year. The recent completion of a new addition has almost doubled our capacity, providing housing for another 25 men. Hundreds of men have been transformed by Christ and established in the Kingdom of God through the ministry of Nehemiah House. Husbands and fathers have been reunited with their wives and children. Other former residents have started successful businesses of their own. Some members of the staff of Nehemiah House, including the current director, are also former residents and participants in the program.

The greatest thing of all, however, is to see many of these men standing in the sanctuary Sunday after Sunday with their hands lifted up and their tears streaming down as they worship their Heavenly Father. Nothing can outdo that! *Does this really work? Absolutely!*

REBUILDING LIVES TO THE GLORY OF GOD

Nehemiah House is named for the Old Testament character Nehemiah, under whose leadership the walls of Jerusalem were rebuilt following the Babylonian Exile. The inspiration for the house is found in Nehemiah's words, "The God of heaven will give us success. We His servants will start rebuilding" (Neh. 2:20b NIV). At the heart of this ministry is a commitment to "rebuilding lives to the glory of God."

Homelessness can happen for any number of reasons. Sometimes a man will run into difficulties at home where his parents or his wife or loved ones will ask him to leave and, with nowhere to go, he ends up on the street. Alcohol or drug abuse can contribute to homelessness when the addictions make it so that a man can't hold a job or pay his rent or keep his life in order. Other men wind up on the street because of emotional problems or psychological disorders. These are only a few of the factors that can cause homelessness.

There are also several stages or degrees of homelessness. The first stage is usually short-term, lasting a few days or weeks before the individual secures a job and/or a place to live. At the next level are the "revolving door" type: homeless who make the rounds from one institution to another, one shelter to another, finding a meal and a place to sleep for a few days at a time, but never being able to get their lives together. The most extreme stage is the homeless who literally live on the street, or in the woods, or in abandoned houses. They are the ones who eat from garbage cans and dumpsters. Many lose their sense of reality. Most are ready to do whatever is required in order to survive.

Nehemiah House is more than just a homeless shelter. It is a *program* and a *ministry* for homeless men. The goal at Nehemiah House is to identify and address with each resident the problems and root causes that led to his homelessness. Our aim is to equip willing men with the tools necessary to help them get out of their homeless condition. We seek to assist them in acquiring gainful employment and a suitable place to live so that they can reestablish themselves in society.

With this in mind, the program at Nehemiah House is structured in three phases.

- *Phase One.* During this 21-day observation phase, residents receive basic life-sustaining care (food and lodging) in a dormitory setting. Many men who enter the house do not advance beyond this phase. Some find a job or a place to live and are no longer homeless. Others break the rules and are asked to leave. Some men choose to leave on their own.

- *Phase Two.* Residents who successfully complete Phase One enter a ten-week (maximum) adjustment phase which focuses on individualized strategies to help them reach their goal of eliminating their homelessness and dependency. With the assistance of staff members, each resident drafts a service agreement plan designed to address his particular situation and needs. During this phase the men learn how to rebuild their self-esteem and refocus their values.

- *Phase Three.* This three-month (maximum) transitional phase is different from the first two phases. The Phase Three resident draws up a new service plan and new goals designed to move him into self-sufficiency and re-entry into society. He takes a more active role and exercises more individual initiative toward realizing his objectives. During this phase the resident becomes involved in the local community, rebuilds his family relationships, and secures employment.

An additional three-month program, the Protective Care Discipleship Program, is available for any resident of Nehemiah House who seeks help in getting free from drug or alcohol addiction. Thoroughly Christ-centered, as is everything at the house, this program is completely voluntary.

In addition to food and shelter, services available to residents of Nehemiah House include attendance at GED and literacy classes, individual counseling and psychological evaluations, recreation and extracurricular activities, medical assistance, and assistance in obtaining employment and benefits. Most important of all, the men are given the opportunity to trust in Christ for salvation and to allow Him to rebuild their lives. Since 1991 literally hundreds of men have been transformed this way. Here are four of them.

LLOYD KIRKLEY

One day in 1996 one of the assistant pastors at Rock City Church received a visitor who was seeking financial help from the church in starting a home business. He was taken by surprise when "Cathy" walked into his office. "Cathy" was in reality Lloyd Kirkley, who had lived for the last three and a half years as a cross-dresser. During all that time Lloyd had never gone anywhere without being dressed as "Cathy."

Even though he was a transvestite, Lloyd was straight and had a girl-friend who thoroughly approved of his cross-dressing. She also thoroughly approved of his money and helped him spend it wildly. When his money ran out, he lost his apartment and moved into a motel. Without money, however, it wasn't long before Lloyd found himself locked out of his room. He was broke and homeless and had nowhere to go. "I knew I wouldn't survive more than a few months on the street," he remembers. Someone recommended that he try to get help from Rock City Church, which is how he ended up in that surprised assistant pastor's office that day.

After talking with Lloyd for a few minutes, the pastor confronted him about his spiritual condition. As Lloyd recalls, "He asked me, 'Have you ever accepted Jesus into your life?' I said, 'No sir, I haven't.' So at that point I was saved. I gave my life to Jesus Christ. Then the pastor made a call to Nehemiah House, and they had a bed for me. That afternoon they took me to Nehemiah House. That was the beginning of a change in my life. I accepted Jesus Christ in my heart, and at Nehemiah House the staff...helped me rebuild my life and change it, and set me on the right track with the Lord."

Lloyd spent one and a half years at Nehemiah House and advanced through Phase Three. Then for about a year he lived in the home of J.D. and Sherry Duval, active members of Rock City Church. During this time he was trying to get approval to receive his Social Security benefits because he had suffered several heart attacks. Lloyd was still waiting to receive his benefits when the Duvals moved to inner-city Baltimore (see

Chapter Nine). Nehemiah House became Lloyd's home again for a couple of months until he received his SSI payments. Then he applied for an apartment through Apartment Search, a service which regularly visits Nehemiah House to assist the residents in finding their own places to live.

Today Lloyd lives in his own apartment and his life is back in order. During his stay at Nehemiah House he fell in love with Jesus and lives now to serve Him. "It's so important," he says, "that people realize that unless you have Jesus Christ, you have nothing. You have to have the Lord in your heart. The Lord has worked a miracle in me. He has turned my life around so much. I have been completely, wonderfully changed by Jesus, and I recommend Him to everybody."

LOU LIKOURGAS

When Lou LiKourgas arrived at Nehemiah House in November 1994, he had been a drug addict for 15 years. Eleven of those years were a very heavy addiction to crack that took complete control of his life. His addiction eventually caused him to become an outcast from his family. They thought he would never amount to anything and wanted nothing more to do with him. Lou ended up on the street, homeless. For awhile he lived in his car. His situation became so grim that he decided to take his life. In fact, he tried to kill himself twice. It was after the second attempt that Lou finally turned to God.

Lou had a sister who was a Christian and who had tried to lead him to Christ years before. By his own admission Lou was too "pigheaded and hardheaded" to receive it. God had to break him in order to humble him so that he would look up.

One November day in 1994 Lou was sitting in his car with a gun he had stolen from a family member. A suicide note lay on the seat next to him. Lou was tired of hurting people who loved him and tired of a life lived solely for the purpose of getting high—a life he could not escape. He cocked the gun and held it to his head, but was unable to pull the trigger. As much as he wanted to die, he couldn't bring himself to go through with it. Something stopped him. Lou now knows that the "something" was God. Dropping the gun in frustration and anger at himself, Lou called out, "Okay, God, if You won't let me take my life, then *You* help me. *You* do something."

With the weather getting colder, Lou knew he needed to find a shelter. It seemed as though every place he called had some reason why they could not take him. Finally, he called Nehemiah House. Three days had passed since Lou had cried out to God while sitting in his car. Nehemiah House had one bed available. Lou says, "I truly believe that bed was left open for me. God heard my cry and answered it. He was there for me. He reached out and saved my life.

"God really worked on me at the Nehemiah House. At first I was stubborn and pigheaded. That was just a little bit of me that was left in me, a little bit of Louie. I allowed God to chisel that away. It was tough. It was hard. Now He's starting to make me into the person I think He wants me to be.

"The structure of the Nehemiah House is what gave me structure in my life. I had none. I had no discipline; no structure. I wasn't going anywhere. I was pretty much at the end of my rope. It taught me a whole new way to live, a better way to live. It set a nice foundation for me to build a chance at a new life."

One of the amazing things God did in Lou's life was open the door for him to start his own business while he was at Nehemiah House. The very first day Lou was there, I called the office looking for qualified painters to paint my new house. Lou had painting experience, and so for the next three months he worked at my house painting. He did such a good job that I contracted with him and another resident of Nehemiah House to paint the new sanctuary of Rock City Church, which was under construction at the time. Out of this experience grew a home improvement business that Lou runs today.

"God works in so many different ways," Lou says. "You're talking about a man who was a homeless, derelict, drug addict and who, three or four months later, is starting his own business. That's an amazing thing. Only God could do something like that."

In the years since he first came to Nehemiah House, Lou has gotten a new lease on life. He has learned how to enjoy life again. Today, life is good for Lou LiKourgas. His business is doing well and he is happily married to a wonderful Christian woman he met at church. He loves the Lord and is quick to share with others what Christ has done for him.

After graduating from Nehemiah House, Lou returned and spent almost a year on the staff there, seeking to help men who were in the same place he had once been in. "It was a great experience to be able to pour back into the lives of the men who were in the same situation that I was before I came to the Nehemiah House. I was able to pour back into their lives and minister to them and witness to them and let them see the actual working of God in me, how God had taken me from a place where they were and put me on the straight and narrow. I was doing the right things. I was going to church on a regular basis. I was living it, actually making it a part of my life, and it was working. I was sticking to it. They saw something in me and I was able to reach a lot of the men. It felt really good that God would send me back to the place where my life was changed to help change someone else's life."

GLENTON TAYLOR

All his life Glenton Taylor had searched for peace. He still remembers a time when he was about five when his heroin-addicted father took him to different women's homes. Glenton would sit at the foot of the bed while his father had sex with the women. On another occasion he witnessed his father stealing the family's Christmas presents. These memories and the burden of trying to hide his father's infidelity from his mother created in Glenton a deep sense of anxiety. This anxiety produced in him a burning desire to achieve.

As Glenton grew up he was always trying to achieve goals, but every goal he reached left him feeling empty inside. He excelled in school, but still felt empty. College was no better. Even though he earned a degree, he still had no inner peace. He did have a drug addiction, however. Hoping to find peace and fulfillment, Glenton had begun drinking when he was 16. By the age of 19 he was snorting cocaine and, by 23, smoking crack. Peace still eluded him.

In desperation, Glenton turned to God. He began reading the Bible. For awhile he would do all right, and then he would backslide. One day his mother told him about Rock City Church. The first day Glenton came was a Tuesday, during one of our "Mary and Martha" conferences. As Glenton remembers, "As I was coming up the hill, I got a great sense of joy. I knew that this was where I was supposed to be. I don't know what happened. I went to the service and all I could do was cry. I went up to the front and prayed. God was there. I just thanked God and I knew that God loved me and that everything was going to be okay."

Afterwards, Glenton went on a tour of the different ministries at the church. When Glenton walked into Nehemiah House, he felt that he was where he belonged. Nevertheless, he went home and kept getting high. He still came to church on occasion, but it was a constant struggle for him. At one point, beginning in April 1998, he went on a three-month binge of getting high and getting drunk. During this time he tried to commit suicide. "I took a bottle of Benadryl, and I woke up three hours later. All I could do was cry and beat the pillow because I was awake; because I was still alive."

After another couple of weeks of getting high and getting drunk, Glenton faced the fact that he could not deal with his problem on his own. He went back to Rock City Church and two weeks later was in Nehemiah House. According to Glenton, being there "got me closer to God. I went to church three or four days a week. I worked at the church every day and I got a sense that I was serving God. They had us pruning gardens and I started to realize that God was pruning me."

Part of the program at Nehemiah House requires residents to save their own money to help them secure their own place to live. Even though Glenton had a college degree, he felt the Lord leading him to seek a job as a janitor. As a result, he found a job the first day he went looking. (The average time for Nehemiah House residents to find a job is two or three weeks.)

During his stay at Nehemiah House, Glenton got off drugs and alcohol, grew closer to the Lord, met his future wife, and saved $6000 in four months, to go toward his own house. Glenton is currently working on his master's degree and expects to finish it by the end of the year.

God has richly blessed Glenton. "By the time I came out of the Nehemiah House, I had a two-bedroom townhouse, money in the bank, and a very good job as a supervisor. Then, about four months out of the program I married a Christian woman. My life is extremely blessed. I no longer worry about how I am going to get this or how I am going to do that. I just give my life to God, and I pray, and I 'seek ye first the Kingdom of Heaven,' and all else shall be mine.

"Before I went to the Nehemiah House, I was always calculating what I needed to do to do this, what I needed to do to get there. Once I gave up and I let go, and stopped being fearful, and I just started praying, and tithing, and being humble toward God, things started working out for me.

"I'd like to thank individuals from the Nehemiah House, but I'm not going to give glory to them by naming their names. Most of all I'd like to thank God for showing me grace in all my life. I should be in jail, or I should be dead, but He has allowed me to continue to live and excel in everything that I've done. I'd also like to thank Him for His mercy and His love. In the name of Jesus Christ, I give Him the glory."

GEORGE HAYNESWORTH

"When God puts you on the right path, He has a plan for your life, and at the end of it you can see His blessings. My life is truly, truly blessed. I have been able to do and accomplish things way beyond anything I could possibly comprehend. This is nothing but God. I was raised strictly 'street,' yet this job has taken me in front of senators, mayors, and legislators, and all sorts of different government agencies. I have been able to tell them about the good news of Jesus Christ and the goodness of God. At the same time, I stress that this is a work to assist the homeless, the ones who have fallen through the cracks of society."

The "job" that George Haynesworth refers to is his current position as the program director of Nehemiah House. It is a remarkable, complete turnaround for a man who first entered Nehemiah House in 1993 after two years on the street. A drug addict, George had reached the most severe form of homelessness, living in the woods, in parking lots, in abandoned houses—wherever he could find a place. He had traveled from state to state by hitchhiking, walking, or hopping freight trains.

George's situation became so hopeless that he was ready to take his own life. That was when he reached out for help. One night when he was alone, trying to sleep under a piece of cardboard, and shaking from "DTs" and the effects of his drug abuse, he called out to God. Even though he was raised on the street, George remembered what his mother had told him years before. "I heard my mom's little voice saying that if I asked Jesus to come into my life, and believed that He would with all my heart, that He would help me and come into my life. That's all I had;

I had nothing else. That night, as I reached out to God, the Holy Spirit came into my life. He allowed me to go back to sleep and stop shaking. God's Word says that He orders the steps of the righteous. From that point on, He had a plan for my life. He had a destiny for me because I made a decision to do what was right, to take Him and bring Him into my life."

The next day George found that he had no urge to drink, even when he was around the same men he had been drinking with for years. That evening George ran into a fellow veteran who took him to a shelter and got him some counseling. From there George spent some time in a VA hospital getting treatment for some injuries to his leg and face. The staff at the VA hospital called Nehemiah House and, because veterans received priority there, George entered the program.

As soon as George arrived at Nehemiah House, he knew he was in a place that was different from other shelters or facilities he had seen. Here the staff listened to the residents' problems and showed genuine love and compassion. They also focused squarely on Christ. The very first night he was there, George had the chance to go to church with staff members and other residents. He knew then that he had found where he needed to be. "I knew in my heart that this is what God had in store for me. When I went to church that night I thanked God for sending me to a place where I could really get myself together. From that point on I applied myself. I knew that this was God's answer to my prayer."

George took advantage of the opportunity to go back to school and get vocational rehabilitation. He enrolled in a two-year computer technology training program, becoming one of only five people out of an original group of 45 to graduate. It was the first time in his life that George had actually completed or accomplished anything significant, and it set him on the path for further accomplishments.

During his nearly two-year stay at Nehemiah House, George also ministered to many of the other residents. "I had hope restored to my life, so I wanted to give that hope to other men. I told them, 'Take advantage of this place. You'll have an opportunity to change your life.' Some of the guys listened to me, and the staff noticed that."

About one and a half months after George graduated from Nehemiah House, he was invited to return as a member of the staff. For the next one and a half years he served as a dorm director. Then, after taking some time off to get married, George returned to Nehemiah House as the program director. Now he has the opportunity to give back some of the blessings God has poured into his life.

Since 1991 hundreds of homeless men have discovered through Nehemiah House the power of Christ to change and rebuild their lives. Nehemiah House has helped them get off drugs, get off alcohol, get off the street, and re-enter society as happy, productive people committed to serving Christ and their fellow man. Only God can bring about such a complete transformation.

Chapter Eight

Helping the Hungry

For I was hungry and you gave Me food; I was thirsty and you gave Me drink (Matthew 25:35a).

Different churches and denominations differ over many things: doctrine, theology, worship style, baptism, the role of the Holy Spirit, you name it. One thing over which there is virtually no disagreement, however, is the church's responsibility to feed the hungry. Christians of every type and "stripe" acknowledge our Lord's commission to take care of the poor and needy. Providing food for the hungry is one of the most basic of ministries. It is non-controversial and non-threatening, and transcends denominational and sectarian walls.

Every person has the right to have enough food to sustain life and health. The United States and all the other major food-producing nations collectively produce more than enough food to provide for the basic nutritional needs of everyone on earth. Yet, every day millions around the world go to bed hungry. Malnutrition and starvation are major health problems in many parts of the world, particularly in Third World countries. Greed, waste, political bureaucracy, and mismanagement all contribute to the problem.

Hunger is not limited to the underdeveloped nations. It is a very real problem right here in our own country, even in our own backyard.

Throughout our land, and particularly in many of our major cities, the number of poor and hungry is growing every day. Many of these are children. Hunger respects no time or seasons. It is a year-round enemy that is as real in July as in December. Any successful approach to feeding the hungry must be more than just a seasonal program. Defeating a year-round enemy requires an aggressive, intense, year-round effort. That is the philosophy and approach behind A Can Can Make a Difference.

It All Began With a Can

During a Sunday night service in 1987 I held up a can of food to remind our people to bring their contributions for the church's food pantry. At the time our food pantry served people both within and outside our congregation who needed food. The pantry needed continual supply, so it was not at all unusual for me to remind our members to bring their cans. I said something about it almost every week. This particular night was no different. Holding up that can of food, I said something like, "Hey, don't forget to give your cans! Remember, a can *can* make a difference."

All of a sudden something broke loose in the church. The response of the congregation was phenomenal. I had never seen anything like it. One of the elders jumped up (something he never did) and said, "I think God is going to give us a soup kitchen one day. Hallelujah!" Then someone else said, "I have a thousand soup bowls I'll donate." (How many people do *you* know who have a thousand soup bowls in their house?) People were standing up one after another all over the sanctuary, saying, "I have towels." "I have paint." "I have a dump truck." "I have a plumber you can use." "I have sheet rock." It went on and on just like that.

Finally I said, "Wait a minute! Hold it! You don't get it! You have just outfitted and remodeled a marvelous building. But we don't own one!" It seemed as though they didn't even hear me; they just kept giving. I was almost in a panic and, not knowing what else to do, I said, "Let's take the offering." That's great pastoral wisdom, you know. When you don't know what else to do, take an offering! You'll get a response of some kind, one way or another. That night about $51,000 came in! I could hardly believe it! Then, turning to a church member who was in the construction business, I asked with a laugh, "Well, brother, do you know of a building? Go find a building for us." (Little did I know that he would pursue it right then!)

After all the excitement had settled down a little I began to preach just as I always did on Sunday night. Suddenly, this same brother walked down to the front of the sanctuary very excited and came right up onto the platform. This kind of behavior was highly out of character for him and I thought, *Either he's about to have a stroke or I'm going to have to let him say something.* As soon as he began to tell his story, it was easy to see why he was so excited.

This brother had left the sanctuary in the middle of the service to make a phone call. Unable to find a phone, he had driven to a phone booth. There he realized that he had no money, since he had given it all in the offering. Nevertheless, he somehow convinced the operator to let him make a free call. The man that he called had just gotten back in town and *just happened* to own a 32,000 square foot building in Baltimore City. At that time it was the largest venetian blind company in the world. Our brother in construction said to him, "We're having a really neat meeting at our church right now and we want you to give us that building." Talk about subtlety!

The man replied, "You know, this is amazing! My wife and I were just sitting here talking about how we need to give this building to a non-profit charitable organization. I can't believe you called! I'll meet you Monday morning."

He *did* meet us Monday morning. Handing me the keys and the title to the building he said, "It's yours." I looked around. There was equipment and heavy machines everywhere. I went over to one machine and pushed the button. A venetian blind shot out. "How about that," I said, "I made a blind." Turning to the (former) owner I asked, "What are you going to do with all this equipment?"

"No," he answered, "the question is what are *you* going to do with it? This is *your* building now, not mine." Just that quickly he walked away from it. We later cut a hole in the roof to remove all the equipment, which sold for thousands of dollars.

Today, that building is the warehouse for A Can Can Make a Difference. Over the years this ministry to feed the hungry has grown phenomenally. Currently, we move and distribute more than seven million pounds of food a year. We do much more than simply feed individual hungry families; we supply soup kitchens and pantries throughout our city as well as up and down the East Coast. God did a sovereign thing that Sunday night in 1987. What began with a can has grown to an operation that utilizes hundreds of volunteers and feeds thousands of people every month. God is so faithful! When we are obedient He responds and does things through us that only He can do.

Making a Difference

Just how serious is the problem of hunger in the United States? It is much more prevalent than most of us realize. Of course, the depth and severity will vary from region to region and state to state, but in general, the number of hungry people in America continues to rise. The city of Baltimore is probably typical of most major urban and metropolitan areas of the country. On any given day there are thousands of people in the city who have no idea where their next meal is coming from. Of the over 800,000 residents of Maryland who are classified as hungry, over 212,000 live in Baltimore City. Another 51,000 reside in Baltimore County. In 1980 there were five soup kitchens in the city of Baltimore; today there are 29, serving an average of 3000 meals a day. Thirty-five food pantries served the needs of Baltimore's hungry in 1980; today over 125 pantries struggle to keep up with the demand.

Compounding the problem is that many of these soup kitchens and food pantries operate on tight budgets. The need to purchase food— even at great discounts—from super pantries or other sources often strains these budgets to the limit. Some of the cost must then be passed down to those to whom the food is distributed. For a destitute mother with three children to feed and who doesn't even have two dimes to rub together, the $4.00 cost for four bags of groceries might as well be $400.00.

A unique feature of A Can Can Make a Difference (CCMAD) is that all the food is distributed *free of charge*, whether given to individuals or, as in most cases, to soup kitchens and food banks to distribute. Since the soup kitchens and food banks receive the food at no cost, they in turn can (and according to CCMAD policy are *required to*) distribute that food at no charge to those who need it.

CCMAD is a community-based program comprised of churches, grocery stores, businesses, corporations, food pantries, soup kitchens, community associations, government agencies, and institutions working together to feed the hungry of Baltimore City, the surrounding counties, and the state of Maryland. It operates through the accumulation in large volume of both perishable and non-perishable food items, which are then dispensed as swiftly and efficiently as possible to every legitimate non-profit food distribution agency. Financial support for CCMAD comes from individual donations, corporate contributions from churches and businesses, and grants.

Food donations come from many different sources: individuals, churches, grocery stores, businesses, reclamation centers. Specific CCMAD collection points are established at churches, grocery stores, and businesses that are enlisted to support the program. At times we even receive truckloads of food that trucking companies have been unable to deliver. Either they received the wrong product or tried to deliver to the wrong place. The sending company does not want to pay to have the goods returned, and the receiving company does not want to pay for goods they did not order. This leaves the trucking company with a load of goods that they must dispose of in some way. At one time the usual solution was simply to throw it away. Now, however, when the shipment involves food items, many of these companies seek to give the food to agencies or organizations that can use it to feed the hungry. Some of these have begun to deliver such shipments to CCMAD.

The CCMAD warehouse serves as a clearinghouse for all food donations. It is a processing center, not a long-term storage facility. Each shipment that arrives is carefully checked in item by item, weighed, and examined for acceptability. Not everything that comes in is usable. Because of breakage, leakage, spoilage, or other factors, 20-30 percent of all the food received by CCMAD must be thrown out. Usable items are stamped for distribution and sent to the sorting table. There they are separated and put into boxes for each food pantry or distribution center we are serving, and then shipped out as soon as possible. The sorting is done in such a way that each customer gets a little bit of everything so that they can have a good variety of food on their shelves to give to the hungry.

Currently, CCMAD regularly supplies over 60 food pantries and distribution centers. We have also begun to expand beyond the borders of the state of Maryland. CCMAD has sent shipments of food to Virginia, North Carolina, Florida, and New York City. Recently, a truckload was shipped to the African nation of Liberia.

Does CCMAD make a difference? Absolutely. Not only are thousands of hungry people being fed every day, but also over the years we have received many testimonies of people who came to Christ as a direct result of receiving help from CCMAD. Lost people often are open and receptive to the gospel of Jesus Christ when their most basic needs—such as hunger—are met by caring, compassionate Christians. Such a ministry is a powerful and undeniable witness to the community. The following two testimonies illustrate the impact a program such as CCMAD can have both on those who participate and those who receive help.

ROSE LONG

At the time of this writing, Rose Long has served as a volunteer at CCMAD for almost eight years. Her burden to feed the hungry goes back much farther. For a long time Rose regularly visited local grocery stores to pick up food to take back to her church to give out to those in the community who were, as she says, "less fortunate than we are." Her compassion is fueled by her love for the Lord and by her gratitude for the blessings He has given her.

One day when Rose visited a grocery store to pick up some food, she met a man from Rock City Church. When he found out that she was gathering food to give to the hungry, he put her in touch with CCMAD. That was the beginning of her association with the program, a relationship that continues today. Although Rose is not a member of Rock City Church, she is a faithful CCMAD volunteer and has attended several of our programs. On occasion, she has even brought groups of youth from her church. About four years ago she helped her church start its own CCMAD program.

Rose says, "The Lord has blessed me so very, very much, because I couldn't understand what my calling was. My calling was, and is, to give [food to] those who are less fortunate than I am; that no woman, child, or senior will go to bed hungry....I have been working with A Can Can Make a Difference for almost eight years, and my life has really, really been blessed. It really doesn't make a difference how old you are, as long as the Lord gives you strength, and the ability to do the thing that He wants you to do....I really want to thank God that He gives me spiritual food to give me the strength to go out and do the thing that I feel that I am supposed to do. For the Lord is good. If it wasn't for the Good Lord above to look down upon me and help me to help somebody else, it could leave me out there looking and watching and waiting for food. I feel this is what I want to do, and I will always do it."

Rev. J.L. Carter

J.L. Carter is pastor of Ark Church, located in east Baltimore. He and his church have been associated with CCMAD ever since they opened a food pantry in 1996. The pantry is a large operation, occupying a two-acre facility. Currently, 12-15 volunteers come each week to ensure that food is picked up, prepared, and distributed to the over 400 *families* that the pantry serves each month. Persons come not only from east Baltimore, but west Baltimore and even from the suburbs to receive food.

Pastor Carter says, "We have a commitment to God's people, both in the church and outside the church. We believe that God is a God who loves everyone, and therefore He has challenged us to love those same people. [CCMAD] has allowed us to fulfill our physical commitment to man. The Church many times focuses on the spiritual commitment, but beyond the spiritual commitment, folks still need a place to live, they still need food to eat, they still need clothes to wear. God has allowed us to begin to address some of those needs. Concerning the food element, we are able to meet that need.

"There are a lot of people who, for some reason or another, are without food to feed their family. Food is expensive. For [CCMAD] to make available this source, this avenue, for receiving food on a weekly basis is a tremendous blessing. I can honestly say that it has helped to keep alive our commitment. At our church we contribute out of our budget. Part of our Sunday morning collections goes towards food, but that is not a large amount of money. If we had to solely depend on that, then we would not be able to service the people that we are. [CCMAD] helps greatly in allowing us to meet the commitment of 400-500 families per month."

The food pantry operated by Pastor Carter and his church has made a significant spiritual impact on those who receive its services. As Rev. Carter shares, "Quite a few unchurched persons come through our lines each week for food. They are awestruck at the fact that a church would go to the lengths to which we do to provide decent, good food. There seems to be a commitment among our workers that they only give out what they would eat themselves, in the sense of it being edible and decent. If it's something that you would not want to eat, then the person in line should not want to eat it either. When you take that kind of care, when you take that kind of love with what you're doing, the unchurched see it, and it becomes the largest example for them at that point in understanding that 'there is really a God somewhere that would make available this for me without cost.'

"Then the same folk come to church and say to me, 'Pastor, I'm here because I was in the line. I was blessed in the line, and I know that I'll be blessed in your church. Any church that can demonstrate that kind of love is the kind of church I need to be a part of.' "

God blesses us to be a blessing. Jesus said, "For everyone to whom much is given, from him much will be required" (Lk. 12:48b). Even something as basic as providing food for the hungry is fundamental to what it means to be Great Commission Christians, dedicated to making disciples in every nation. Feeding the hungry is being like Jesus, who would not send the multitudes away with empty stomachs, but gave them bread and fish. When we feed people in Jesus' name, they see His love and grace at work in us and are drawn to Him.

Chapter Nine

One Block at a Time

Your people will rebuild the ancient ruins and will raise up the age-old foundations; you will be called Repairer of Broken Walls, Restorer of Streets with Dwellings (Isaiah 58:12 NIV).

ack in Chapter Three I said that God has a heart to redeem and restore our cities because He loves people, and cities are where most people are found. Before the cities can be restored, however, the Church must be restored. When God restores His people, He plants in them *His* heart, *His* desires, and *His* purpose. For this reason, churches that have been restored by the Spirit and power of God will also have a heart to reclaim and restore their cities.

If God desires to restore the cities and bring people to Himself, it stands to reason that He would have a plan for doing so. Is there a biblical pattern for restoring cities and reclaiming them for the Lord? I believe there is. The Old Testament Book of Nehemiah provides a model for just such a restoration. It is not necessarily the *only* biblical model, but it is certainly a good one. Adopt-A-Block, the organized and deliberate approach that we use at Rock City Church for restoring the city of Baltimore one block at a time, is inspired by and patterned after the Nehemiah model.

RESTORING HIS CITY

Nehemiah was a Jew who lived in Persia in the fifth century BC during the years immediately following the period of Jewish captivity known as the Babylonian Exile. He served in the important and influential position of cupbearer to the king of Persia. This was an office of trust, tasting the king's wine and food to protect the king from any who might try to poison him. As such, it required discernment, courage, and character. Nehemiah had all of these in abundance. Because of his intimate daily ministering to the king, Nehemiah had both the king's trust and the king's ear.

Although Nehemiah was born in exile, as a faithful and devout Jew his heart was always toward the city of Jerusalem and his ancestral homeland. When he received the news that the city lay in ruins and its walls destroyed, he was deeply moved. Nehemiah wept over the condition of his city. He knew that it was the sin of his people that had led to God's judgment, their captivity, and the destruction of Jerusalem. Under deep conviction, Nehemiah identified with and confessed the sins of his people. He fasted, prayed, and poured his heart out in intercession for them and for his city (see Neh. 1:3-11). Like Nehemiah, we too must begin with a godly burden for our city if we hope to see it restored according to God's purpose.

Stirred to action by the Spirit of God and by his burden for Jerusalem, Nehemiah appealed to the king for permission to go to Jerusalem and rebuild the walls of the city. In his holy boldness he even requested from the king a letter authorizing the work. Furthermore, he had the audacity to ask for money from the king's own treasury to pay for the reconstruction! God's favor rested upon Nehemiah, because the king granted each request, and even provided a military escort (see Neh. 2:1-9). When we seek under God's leadership to restore our city, He will give us favor in the eyes of government officials and make government resources available for the work.

Nehemiah was a skilled administrator, apparently possessed ample engineering knowledge, and was an inspiring and effective leader. The first thing he did upon arriving in Jerusalem was to survey the damage to the city and the ruins of the walls. Then he gathered all the leaders of the people, both civic and religious, and challenged them with his burden and commission from the Lord to rebuild the walls of the city. The leaders and officials accepted Nehemiah's challenge, and together they set to work (see Neh. 2:12-18). Restoring our cities requires the cooperative effort of many different people. No individual, no one group, no single church can do it alone.

Despite opposition from enemies opposed to God's work, Nehemiah and the people of Jerusalem and the surrounding area completed the wall in 52 days—a clear sign of God's blessing and supernatural enablement upon His plan and His servants. It was a cooperative effort involving people of every social class and walk of life—everyone who had a love for and devotion to their city:

- Nehemiah, the administrator and overseer
- Priests (local pastors)
- The people (local congregations)
- Governors, rulers, and officers (government officials and agencies)
- Soldiers (law enforcement)
- Merchants (businessmen and private enterprise)
- Carpenters, masons, apothecaries, goldsmiths, and other artificers (tradesmen)
- Fathers and families (city residents)

In the great task of restoring the city there was work and a place for everyone. Some gave oversight, some labored, and some contributed financially. One significant fact is that each priest (pastor) repaired the wall and restored the breach in front of his own house (church)! "Beyond the Horse Gate the priests made repairs, each in front of his own house" (Neh. 3:28). Each priest (pastor) was responsible for his own "block"!

Everyone joined efforts and combined resources to help one another. The work was systematic, with each group laboring in their respective communities. By working in harmony with one another and standing side by side, they closed the breaches in the wall. The project succeeded because an all-volunteer labor force was absolutely committed to the restoration of their neighborhoods. The people had a mind to work.

Underlying the physical restoration of a city or neighborhood is the goal of the spiritual restoration of the people who live there. Ezra rebuilt the temple in Jerusalem and, a generation later, Nehemiah rebuilt the walls of the city to fortify it. In a similar way, after a person is born again of the Spirit and God's "temple" is restored in his body, then the "wall" of his personality and soul (mind, emotions, and will) can be restored.

Biblical ministry is ministry to the whole man, both natural and spiritual. In the natural, breaches and gaps are restored in physical dwellings, possessions, finances, and even physical health and appearance. In the spiritual realm, gaps in the human personality—emotional hurts and traumas, rejection, guilt, fear, complexes, mental disorders, identity crises, and the like—are healed in the Spirit. This is the true restoration that God desires to bring to our cities. It can be accomplished only through the leading and empowering of the Holy Spirit.

Adopt-A-Block

Adopt-A-Block is a partnership comprised of local churches, city government, the police department, local businesses, community services, community associations, health agencies, and local residents working together to bring restoration to our inner city block by block. The goal is to meet the diversified spiritual, emotional, mental, and physical needs of individuals, families, and communities.

At the center of the Adopt-A-Block approach is the block party, where we "adopt" an entire city block with all its residents, and provide various types of assistance and opportunities to help them improve their living conditions. Block residents find free clothing and groceries available, along with job counseling and placement, housing improvements, educational opportunities, drug counseling, health care screenings and checkups, and sports programs. Music is an important part of each event, and every party ends with the preaching of an evangelistic message. In addition, trained witnesses mill through the crowd seeking to share Christ one-on-one with partygoers as they have opportunity.

The strategy of Adopt-A-Block is to systematically recover a city or district block by block. First, a block is identified and targeted for invasion and conquest. Then, that block is occupied, or "adopted." Once the block has been secured and is in the process of restoration, another block is chosen and the cycle repeats until the entire city or district is restored. If you think this sounds like a military campaign, it is in a way.

The reason so many of our cities are in such deep trouble, despair, and deterioration is because they are in the grip of demonic strongholds that strive to keep people in spiritual darkness and hopelessness. These forces are deeply entrenched and will not surrender without a fight. Adopt-A-Block is more than cosmetic surgery to a neighborhood or surface social reform. At heart it is all-out spiritual warfare.

The block party is only the beginning, however. Critical to the long-term success of Adopt-A-Block is the involvement of the local churches. Follow-up is essential, and no one is better suited or positioned to do it than the congregations that are physically located in the "adopted" geographical area. For this reason, we enlist the support of the local church and pastor in the earliest stages of planning any Adopt-A-Block event. As block residents are won to Christ they are welcomed into the neighborhood churches and discipled into mature believers. The end result of all this effort is a community that has new hope with a renewed sense of self-worth and purpose.

City government with all its programs and agencies alone cannot bring restoration to our cities. At best, even the most efficient and innovative programs have seen only marginal success. The police department and other local law enforcement agencies can enforce the law and protect citizens, but they lack the ability to bring about genuine change. Education is important, but it too is unable to stand alone against the epidemic growth of despair in our cities. Only the Church possesses the wisdom, power, and spiritual resources necessary to bring deliverance and true restoration to our cities.

There are six parts of society in every city that have to be penetrated by the Church for true city transformation to take place:

- Political—Through prayer and action as Nehemiah did, we must influence and help our local political officials.

- Educational—There has to be a break in the old mind-set of church and state rules. Beginning in kindergarten and continuing through college, the Church has to prayerfully and deliberately engage itself in the schools of our inner cities—from before-school prayer, to after-school care programs, to PTA involvement. People perish for a lack of knowledge! (See Hosea 4:6.)

- Church—Unity commands the blessing of the Lord! There are more gangs (groups, denominations) in the church world than have ever been on the streets of our cities. Second Chronicles 29:16 tells how King Hezekiah restored the temple by first removing the debris from the inner part of the temple. We must remove the debris of past suspicions, hurts, and racial and ethnic differences. We must come together to rebuild our cities.

- Law enforcement—The New Testament tells us that God has placed in authority those who pass and enforce our laws—the courts, police, and juvenile authorities (see Rom. 13:1). We must reach in and prayerfully influence and help them. Rock City Church has been able to establish a worship service that meets every Thursday night in the Baltimore city police headquarters. By first breaking down the walls that keep us out of an active role in legislation and law enforcement, we can restore and build the right walls of strength and defense for our communities and cities.

- Media—Words have tremendous power for good or evil. Nehemiah's enemies Sanballat and Tobiah sent intimidating words throughout the city, trying to stop or hinder his work (see Neh. 4:1-6:14). But the Church can penetrate the electronic or printed media for the Kingdom of God. The media can publish a good report and change the atmosphere of our cities. In Baltimore we've seen the media help the efforts of the Church.

- Financial—A quote I heard years ago is, "He who has the gold rules." Whoever has the money or the authority over the money has the power to rule in our cities, our communities, and our nation. The Church in this country has been weak for so long because we have very little provision for our visions. Proverbs 13:22 says, "...the wealth of the sinner is stored up for the righteous." Nehemiah found the resources to rebuild Jerusalem in the riches of the king who held his people captive (see Neh. 2:7-9). Joseph spared Egypt and his own people by being in charge of the wealth. Moses took gold and silver from Egypt and used it to build the tabernacle in the wilderness. David took the spoils from his enemies to build the temple of

God. We must change our old mind-sets about going to the world to get funds. From businesses to grants and private donations—the finances are available to rebuild cities. At Rock City Church we have a full-time grant writer on staff. Through his efforts we have received, over the past ten years, several million dollars from various sources. Getting this money has never, not even once, hindered us from preaching the gospel.

It is time for the churches in the cities to rise and meet the challenges that are set before us. For too long the Church has neglected the true, biblical, "full gospel" commission of our Lord to not only preach salvation and deliverance to the captives, but also to clothe the naked, feed the hungry, and shelter the homeless. Success will come as the churches in a given location learn how to work together to win back their communities. Psalm 133:1 says that the Lord commands His blessing where brothers (and sisters) dwell together in unity. Under the leadership of churches empowered by the Holy Spirit, the working partnership with the government and the private and business sectors will form an irresistible force against the strongholds that have our cities in a death grip.

Through Adopt-A-Block we seek to

- Systematically recover our city from poverty, oppression, hopelessness, crime, and drugs, block by block.

- Promote unity and a working relationship among local churches.

- Address the physical needs of an individual home or block of homes.

- Raise awareness of inner city needs in the private and business sectors of the community and provide defined opportunities for their involvement and assistance.

- Provide a resource center for churches and partnership agencies.

One of the important follow-up strategies of Adopt-A-Block is to acquire a house within the adopted area either through purchase or donation. The house is renovated as needed, and then a trained, spiritually mature and committed Christian family moves in. They create a permanent presence in the neighborhood for spiritual influence, counsel, and assistance for the rest of the block. The testimony that follows is from a couple who live with their children in one of these houses as neighborhood inner-city missionaries.

J.D. AND SHERRY DUVAL

Since May 1999 J.D. Duval has been the director of A Can Can Make a Difference. Almost a year earlier, in July 1998, J.D. and his wife Sherry gave up life as they had known it, left their nice home in a peaceful neighborhood, and moved with their two children into a row house on a street in inner-city Baltimore. At the time of their arrival, drug dealing was active on both ends of their block. Even one of their neighbors was selling drugs. During the first six months after they moved in, five or six murders occurred in the neighborhood, most of them drug-related. The sound of gunfire was a common occurrence. People, even young children, were outside on the streets at all hours of the day or night.

What would motivate a young Christian family to trade the peace and security of suburbia for the unrest and turmoil of an inner-city neighborhood? It was neither a quick nor impulsive decision for the Duvals, but rather the outworking of a burden that had been growing in their hearts for several years.

Shortly after their marriage nearly six years ago J.D. and Sherry began dreaming of the kinds of things they could do to reach out and minister to people if they lived in the inner city. Their dreams developed into a burden, which grew into a burning desire. J.D. recalls, "We had no idea where we were going. God just opened up the doors. When the opportunity came for us to move down into the city, my wife and I just looked at each other in amazement that the time was here. We had talked about this for years. It was so heavy on our hearts that we ran down to the front of the church after the pastor announced that there was an opening coming up. We wanted to be first in line. It turned out that we were the only ones in line. People are too afraid to go down into the city where it is dangerous. But this was on our hearts. We were excited, we were like little kids with a new bike.

"The pastor asked us to put something together. My logistical wife went to work on the paperwork and showed him what our plans were and what we wanted to do. He was so excited that he pressed forward and we moved into one of the houses on Adopt-A-Block."

During the first two weeks they were there, the Duvals took three neighborhood children sailboating in the bay. J.D. and Sherry had met a man who owned a 38-foot sailboat, and he took them out. They spent the night on the water and sailed around the bay for several hours the next day. None of the three neighborhood children had ever been on a boat before, and everybody had a great time.

Not every experience was this pleasant, however. As J.D. relates, "In February [1999], one of the drug dealers got mad at us and torched our car. We came home from a Tuesday night service, worshiping and praising God. We were dancing before God all night long. By the time we got home we were so lit that in essence we basically laughed when we found out that somebody had torched our car. The police had the street blocked off and our kids were asking, 'What's going on?' Sherry said, 'Somebody torched our car.' One of the kids said, 'Why would they do that?' She said, 'I guess maybe they're trying to scare us out.' Our daughter crossed her arms over her chest and said, 'If they think that's all it's going to take to move us out, they've got another thing coming, 'cause we ain't going!' "

Within a week a family in the church gave the Duvals a used Cadillac to replace the car that had burned. It was quite a testimony to the neighborhood that God is indeed a great provider. People in the neighborhood began approaching the Duvals to express their sorrow over what had happened as well as their gladness that the incident had not scared them into moving away.

About a month later, the drug dealer who had torched their car suddenly dropped dead of a blood clot in his leg. J.D. says, "We were not really happy with that; we really wanted him to get saved. We were hoping for a salvation, but he didn't make it. The rest of the neighborhood knew what had happened. From that day, drugs aren't being sold on our street anymore. They're sold up the street and down the street, but they're not sold on our street.

"Neighbors have come up and told us how peaceful the neighborhood has become since we moved in. It's not us; it has nothing to do with us. If it were me, I would have never moved down there. It's God. God is the one who called us to move down there. God is the one who has brought peace into the neighborhood. God is the one who orchestrates everything. We are responsible for responding to His ability."

According to J.D., living among the people of the neighborhood is critical to effective ministry to them. "Shortly after we moved down there, God spoke to me and told us that there was no way we could ever minister to these people if we didn't live there. We could be there eight hours, ten hours a day, but unless we lived in the neighborhood, unless we lived next door to them, there was no way that we could ever minister to them. We would have no idea what they go through or what their lives are like."

Sherry adds, "I remember when we were first there. All you have to do is go and sit on your steps. All the kids are out on the street, all day, all night long. Sometimes at 2:00 in the morning when you come home the kids would be out running. The doors would be locked, they couldn't get in their houses, their moms weren't around; the kids were just running. I would go and sit on our steps and the girls would come and climb in my lap, look at my fingers, and ask me what my wedding rings were. They didn't even know what wedding rings were. Another time they would ask us what our last names were. It was just amazing to them that the four of us all had the same last name. That's not very common in the inner city in those lifestyles.

"The race factor has never been an issue. When you go down and people know you accept them and love them and don't judge them, they see you as one of them, and color has nothing to do with it. One day our daughter was sitting on the step with one of the girls and a white man came into the neighborhood and was knocking on a door. The girl from the neighborhood said, 'What does that white man think he's doing down here?' Our daughter said, 'Well, what about us?' The other girl said, 'Oh, you don't count. You're black, too. You're just one of us.' It's an awesome thing to see that unity can come and prejudice go away when love exists. It's not us, because it would be a fake thing. It's God."

One day J.D. went outside and found two young boys ages 11 and 9, just wandering the streets. Their mother was a cocaine and heroin user and had not been around for about three days. At first, the boys had stayed with their aunt, but when they made her mad she brought them home and dropped them off in the street to fend for themselves with no supervision. The boys' house had no heat, and no electricity. During the mother's absence someone had broken into the house, stolen the refrigerator and stove, and sold them.

J.D. brought the boys inside and they had a great time sleeping on the living room floor in sleeping bags. Even though the boys had effectively been abandoned, the Duvals didn't want to call the police and see the boys end up in the system. The Duvals took the boys to church, and when they got home J.D. walked up to the boys' house. This time, their mother was there. As Sherry remembers, "She came down, and she was a mess. She had been using [drugs] straight for three or four days, and she couldn't look us in the face, couldn't eat anything. She was crying. We prayed with her and talked with her. Then we laid hands on her. She repented and she got saved. Then we prayed a prayer of deliverance and she fell out of her chair and was rolling on the floor, back and forth. J.D. just spoke peace into her, and all of a sudden her countenance changed. We knew that the spirit of addiction had left because she was laughing and had joy in her life. She got up and was a transformed woman. She was eating, she was laughing, she could look at us; it was just amazing to us. We had never seen anything like this before. We knew that God did things like this, but we had never before been personally involved this way."

The Duvals have hosted Christmas parties in their home with as many as 30 neighborhood kids there. They make up bags of food and candy for the families and presents for the children. Living in the inner city has become their life. They can't imagine ever going back to the life they used to live. Sherry says, "We thought we were going to be such a blessing, but every time we open our hearts, and we open our house up to the neighbors and to these kids, we find that we're the ones that God has so richly blessed. There is such satisfaction in what we do."

J.D. and Sherry Duval have discovered the secret of reaching the inner city: person by person, house by house, block by block, by demonstrating the love of Christ through long-term personal commitment of themselves and their resources as they live day by day among the people that God has given them a heart to reach. This is also the philosophy behind Adopt-A-Block. So far, we have "adopted" over 40 blocks, with three or four new ones targeted every year. Our goal is to continue in this way until the entire city is reclaimed from the clutches of the enemy, and the people of the city brought into the light of Christ. We believe that this is the New Testament way to "seek our brothers."

Chapter Ten

A Church for the New Millennium

Behold, I will do a new thing, now it shall spring forth; shall you not know it? I will even make a road in the wilderness and rivers in the desert (Isaiah 43:19).

At the brink of a new millennium, the Christian Church faces unprecedented challenges. Changes in our society and our culture demand a different response from the Church. Traditional methods, attitudes, and practices of the past by and large are no longer sufficient. There was a time when the Church was the primary source of care and help for the needy of society. Somewhere along the way we gradually surrendered that role to government agencies and welfare programs. Today, in many ways, the lost world does a better job of caring for the needy than the Church does. As James wrote, "My brothers, this should not be" (Jas. 3:10b NIV).

Although we would never wish to admit it, when it comes to reaching out to society's "throw-aways," "the ones that nobody wants," the contemporary Church too often exhibits the attitude of Cain. After Cain murdered his brother Abel, the Lord confronted him with his deed. "Then the Lord said to Cain, 'Where is Abel your brother?' He said, 'I do not know. Am I my brother's keeper?' " (Gen. 4:9) That's the question the Church must reexamine as we face the 21st century. *Are we our brother's keeper?*

The answer to that question, from both the words and example of Jesus, is yes. As our Elder Brother (see Rom. 8:29), Jesus came "to seek and to save that which was lost" (Lk. 19:10b). He is the Shepherd who leaves the 99 sheep safe in the fold and goes off "to seek the one that is straying" (Mt. 18:12b). He is the Son of Man who is not afraid or ashamed to be called "a friend of tax collectors and sinners" (Mt. 11:19b). He is the Great Physician who came to heal sick sinners and call them to repentance (see Mk. 2:17b).

Just as Jesus *came* seeking us, we are to *go*, seeking *our* brothers. As never before, this is the challenge of the Church of the new millennium. We cannot seek our brothers and maintain an exclusive mind-set. Most of us, within a few years of becoming a Christian, no longer have any lost friends. The only people we hang around with are other Christians. In our churches we tend to seek others who are like ourselves: same ethnic background, same educational level, same socio-economic class. We will never reach the lost unless we go out among them. If we hope to bring in the "ones nobody wants," we cannot hold them at arm's length. We must be willing to *touch* them.

REACH OUT AND TOUCH SOMEONE

Once again, Jesus is our supreme example. He never hesitated to violate social custom or tradition if it meant He could touch someone in need.

> *When He had come down from the mountain, great multitudes followed Him. And behold, a leper came and worshiped Him, saying, "Lord, if You are willing, You can make me clean." Then Jesus put out His hand and touched him, saying, "I am willing; be cleansed." Immediately his leprosy was cleansed. And Jesus said to him, "See that you tell no one; but go your way, show yourself to the priest, and offer the gift that Moses commanded, as a testimony to them"* (Matthew 8:1-4).

In the society of Jesus' day there was no more dreaded disease than leprosy. The Law stipulated that lepers had to maintain a strict distance from other people and call out "Leper!" as a warning to them to stay away. Anyone who touched a leper was immediately considered unclean.

Lepers were condemned to a life of solitude, objects of revulsion, forever denied the warmth of human touch or affection.

It is particularly significant, therefore, that Jesus *touched* this leper as He healed him. To society he was an outcast, yet Jesus touched him. To the self-righteous of the day his leprosy was God's judgment for his sins, yet the Son of God touched him. Many were the times that Jesus healed with merely a word: the centurion's servant (see Mt. 8:5-13), the paralytic on his mat (see Mt. 9:2-7), blind Bartimaeus (see Mk. 10:46-52). With the leper, however, Jesus healed with a word and a *touch*. Jesus knew how starved this man was simply for human contact. Such a simple gesture of compassion as a touch was as healing to the leper's spirit as the divine power was to his body. When Jesus touched the leper, He defied every social and *religious* custom of His day. In doing so, however, He restored a man to wholeness, both body and spirit. A "throwaway," an outcast, one of those whom nobody wanted, was reclaimed for the Kingdom of God; a lost brother was brought home.

Today, there are "lepers" all around us. They are easy to see if we will simply open our eyes and look. They are the ones society has written off as hopeless or unworthy of attention. Worse still, they are the ones that many *churches* have written off as well.

The challenge of reaching these people calls for a radically new and different Church, or perhaps simply a radical return to the pattern and practice of the New Testament Church. As I have stressed throughout this book, in these days God is raising up a radical new generation of believers—the Joseph generation—to be the heart and soul of a restored Church for a new millennium. Impatient with the status quo and not content automatically to do things the old way, this company of saints will not be afraid to buck tradition in order to carry out God's mandate to reach the nations. This will extend even to touching those whom society, tradition, and "religion" say we should not touch. When we allow God to strip away the trappings of tradition and religion that cause us to separate ourselves from the "undesirables," we will begin to see them the way Jesus does, and begin to treat them the way He did. *The Church of the new millennium will be a touching Church.*

REUNION OF MARY AND MARTHA

God is redefining His Church. He is raising up a Joseph generation, placing people in designated places, for a particular time, at the end of an age, and for a specific purpose. That purpose is to provide both naturally and spiritually all that is needed to preserve and to restore to Himself our cities, our nation, and ultimately, our world.

Over the past three years we at Rock City Church have come to understand the balance between the natural and the spiritual provision more than ever before. As I mentioned in Chapter One, the coming of the awesome presence of God in our church beginning in January 1997 brought with it a fresh understanding of the relationships that Martha and Mary had with Jesus. These two close friends of Jesus learned how to minister to both His physical and spiritual needs. As the practical-minded one with a servant's heart, Martha took particular delight in meeting Jesus' physical needs, such as food and drink or a place to sleep. Martha knew and loved Jesus as her Messiah, but her special gift was hosting His *humanity*. In Martha we see a heart of *compassion* for people's needs.

Mary, on the other hand, found her greatest joy in sitting at Jesus' feet, worshiping and adoring Him, and hanging on His every word. Mary knew how to host Jesus' *deity*. Her heart was full of *passion* for her Lord.

Because Martha and Mary knew how to minister to Jesus' total needs, body and spirit, He felt more comfortable in their home in Bethany than He did anywhere else. He was revered, honored, loved, and cared for. No wonder that Jesus chose to stay there whenever He was in Bethany! They made Him feel welcome.

Martha represents the natural and Mary represents the spiritual. Both are vital. Both are a part of everyday life, of humanity at its core. In January 1997 God began to show us that if the churches ever get Martha and Mary together again under the same roof, then everything that is dead (Lazarus) in our cities will start to come alive.

For years, ever since I came to Baltimore, I have sought ways to bring pastors and churches of the city together to promote unity and to cooperate in common efforts. There have been some successes, but mostly on a small scale. Since the revival began however, the door to unity has opened much wider. Over the past three years we have seen pastors from all over the city, from across the country, and from around the world attend our meetings.

When people are hungry for God, denominational barriers fall and doctrinal differences fade. All that matters is being in His presence. I am now seeing a much greater interest among Baltimore pastors in working together than I did before. I am convinced that this new interest is the result not only of the greater manifest presence of God in our church but also the years of sowing and ministering and working that we have done in the city. God has shown us His favor and is bringing about His purpose in the fullness of time. It is "Martha" and "Mary" working *together*, as it should be.

Most churches today favor one or the other, rarely both in equal measure. One church will have a strong *passion* for Jesus with dynamic praise and worship, and that will be their focus. Another will build its ministry around *compassion* for people in need. Why can't we do both? That's the Church that Jesus established, and the one that He is restoring in our generation. Unless both *passion* and *compassion* are present, any church is incomplete and underdeveloped.

Whenever a church manages to put the two together, however, the result is an incredibly powerful witness. Two is the number of witness. In Old Testament law, the testimony of two witnesses was required to determine the truth of a matter in court. People naturally will be drawn to a congregation that has a passion for worship, a passion for prayer, a passion for holy living, and a passionate love for God and His Word and who at the same time channel their passion into compassionate acts of ministry and service.

Like Egypt in the days of Joseph, there is famine in our land. It is not so much a famine of food, although there are certainly plenty of hungry people. It is a famine of hope, a famine of joy, a famine of peace, a famine of morality and righteousness. People all over our land are desperate to know that tomorrow can be better than today and that life is more than a daily cycle of discouragement, despair, and desperation. When they see the *presence* of God and experience the *love* of God through the lives of the *children* of God, they receive hope.

With the coming of revival in our church, God has reunited "Martha" and "Mary." He has opened our eyes as never before to the element of *passion* for the Lord as the fuel for everything we do. God has wedded *passion* and *compassion* once again. There will not be another divorce. What God has joined together, man will not tear asunder. I believe that this is the pattern for the Church of the new millennium, and those who are of the Joseph generation will be at its heart.

THE ONE EVERYBODY IS AFTER

For over 16 years at Rock City Church God let us build a strong base in one particular arena, compassion ministries. Then, a little more than three years ago, God showed up in power and revealed to us a whole new dimension regarding passion. Although we already had a degree of passion for the Lord, the revival took us to a whole new level.

At first, I was a little worried that the outreach ministries that we have done for years would suffer. I was concerned that many of our people would get so caught up in lying on the floor, weeping and seeking a touch from the Lord, that they would retreat into the prayer closet and never come out again. My fears were unfounded. After only a short time, the presence of God in revival infused into people's hearts a greater passion for Him. As their passion for God increased, so did their compassion to touch men.

I discovered in my own experience that whenever we have trouble loving other people, it is because we really are not in love with God. The apostle John stated it this way, "If someone says, 'I love God,' and hates his brother, he is a liar; for he who does not love his brother whom he has seen, how can he love God whom he has not seen?" (1 Jn. 4:20) When we are in love with God, we can't help but love man, because man was created in God's image and for His purpose. So the two really work together. When we are in love with God, we want to be like Him and do something that is God-like. How do we know what God is like? We look to Jesus, because when we see Him we see the Father. Seeing Jesus, we seek to do the things He did. What did Jesus do? He showed compassion, extended mercy, and reached out to those who needed help and hope.

This is nothing more than the fulfillment of what Jesus identified as the two greatest commandments: to love God with all our heart, soul, mind, and strength, and to love our neighbor as ourselves (see Mt. 22:37-40). Those who have a hot passion for God will have a difficult time turning a cold shoulder to people in need. You can't very well spend time with God and then ignore the broken, the desperate, the hungry, the homeless, and the *lost* whom you pass by on the street every day.

Reaching out to men without a deep love for God in our hearts can lead to discouragement and burnout because the demands are great and will pull at us and drain us. When love for God is at the center of all we do, we will find that He renews our strength, gives us His rest, and fills us with His love, so that we can easily sustain and love people who are unloved.

Years ago, when the Lord said to me, "If you will take care of the ones that nobody wants, I will give you the ones everybody is after," I thought He meant the kind of people that most churches are after: doctors, lawyers, and people with money and prestige. All people are important in God's eyes, but one reason the Church has been so weak and ineffective is because so often we have sought out the "uppity-ups" to the exclusion of the "down-and-outs." What we discovered in January 1997, however, is that God Himself came in. *He* is "the One everybody is after." In effect, He said, "If you will take care of the ones that nobody wants, *I'll* come in." That's just what He did. He came in and has kept on coming. Instead of our social ministries suffering, they have multiplied. God came in and brought the increase. He is grooming us for the harvest.

THE COMING REVIVAL

I am convinced that our nation is headed for a great revival. All the signs are in place. There is moral and ethical decline on an unprecedented scale. In practical terms most Americans reject God and ignore His Word (if they even know it). Yet, God is beginning to stir His people. These are the same conditions that have existed immediately prior to every significant revival on record. Moral and spiritual decline is followed by moral renewal, spiritual growth, and a great increase in general prosperity. One key factor in every revival is the reaching of the poor and the destitute.

Karl Marx wrote *Das Kapital*, his great thesis on communism, out of anger in London during a time of great famine. More than thirty thousand children were on the streets. Three of Marx's own children died of starvation and malnutrition. Marx was angry at the lack of passion in the institutional Church and its failure to care for the needy. At the same time that Marx was writing, D.L. Moody was preaching and ministering in the city. God used Moody to bring revival to England. A time of physical and spiritual famine was replaced by a time of physical and spiritual prosperity.

In the past we have had program evangelism. John Wimber taught us about power evangelism. Now we are entering the day of what Tommy Tenney calls "presence evangelism." This means going into the street, or into a bar, or into a jail, or into a drug-infested area with the glory of God on you. The Book of Acts tells how Peter's shadow fell on people and healed them. I believe that this shadow wasn't caused by the sun, but was a sense of the glory of God that rested on Peter.

Since January 1997 we have seen the same presence and power of God that happens in church happen right out on the street during our block parties. People are being saved by the hundreds and experiencing the fullness of the Spirit. As a church we are learning that it really is okay to take Jesus outside of the four walls. I don't know where it came from, but somehow, somewhere many of us have gotten the idea that the only place Jesus likes to be is in church. I'm sorry, but judging from the New Testament, Jesus spent less time in church than He did anywhere else. I am convinced that one of the reasons He is absent from so many of our churches is because He doesn't like what we've done to them. That's why He is working now to restore His Church and bring His people back to Himself.

If we create a true house of worship, He will show up. That's what He is looking for. At the same time, He loves being out there with Bartimaeus and Zacchaeus and with lepers and demoniacs—anywhere there are people in need. The Church must love what He loves. We must cultivate a passion for both. It is already beginning to happen in many places.

I have a dream that somewhere in some shopping mall, or on some street, or in a state house or other government building somewhere, the glory of God will fall with such power that it will make the nightly news. There are already several places around the world where entire cities are being turned around to God. I believe that God wants to show up everywhere. I'm the kind of guy who believes that God can show up at Starbucks, or at Sears, or at the football game.

The Church of the new millennium is one that will break out of the four walls and invade the streets and the neighborhoods, the businesses and the factories, the schools and the government houses. It will exalt the name of Jesus, who said, "And I, if I am lifted up from the earth, will draw all peoples to Myself" (Jn. 12:32). Like King David with the Ark of the Covenant we will walk and dance in the streets, rejoicing that the glory of God is returning to the city. He is raising up the Joseph generation for just such a day as this. Old things are passing away; a new day is dawning.

> *Behold, I will do a new thing, now it shall spring forth; shall you not know it? I will even make a road in the wilderness and rivers in the desert* (Isaiah 43:19).

Appendix A

The Hiding Place

THE MISSION STATEMENT

To help a woman who finds herself alone in a crisis pregnancy or crisis situation, by providing housing, clothing, food, prenatal care, and genuine love and concern in a family atmosphere.

STARTING A HIDING PLACE

This manual is a guideline for establishing a crisis pregnancy home in your area. When starting a home, it is important to have a passion for the work and for the women who need to be reached. The following points should be considered:

1. Submit the vision to the pastor overseeing the concept.
2. Determine the need.
3. Inquire about existing programs that have established funds.
4. Research pregnancy homes and crisis centers in your area to determine the population that needs targeting.
5. Raise up a person willing to operate the program.
6. Find a suitable location for the home with proper zoning to build and operate.

STATEMENT OF PURPOSE

1. To provide a Christ-centered family setting in which women in need may find the love of a family and discover the love of Jesus.

2. To lead women into a loving relationship with the living God and to assist them in their early Christian growth.
3. To provide women with the necessary food, clothing, and medical care for their physical well-being.
4. To offer counsel and love to women, their babies, families, and the alleged father (if possible), in a caring atmosphere which will help the women grow in their relationships.
5. To offer unbiased and loving counsel concerning the welfare of the baby and mother.
6. To encourage continuing education during the women's stay by fostering a positive attitude towards education and learning.
7. To assist the women in adjusting back into a family structure or into an independent living situation when they leave the home, always maintaining a bond of love, prayer, and communication with them.
8. To help build self-esteem and install moral character in the women.

ORGANIZATION AND ADMINISTRATION

The board is the advisory committee for the organization.

I. **Board Members Job Descriptions**
   A. *President*
      1. To establish and define the purpose, direction, and vision for the home.
      2. To establish personnel policies, living arrangements, definition of duties, and performance standards and evaluations.
      3. To appoint leaders to administer and give leadership to the home.
      4. To approve all budgets and administrative costs that are set for the home.
      5. To oversee management of the funds and properties of the home in order to track spending.
      6. To assist the appointed leaders in prayerful, godly direction for the women, while they are in the home and upon their leaving the home.
      7. To assist and always be clearly advised on any situation with both the home and/or the women, which could have potential negative effects on the overall ministry of the home.
      8. To call and conduct all board meetings, and to appoint and remove board members.
   B. *Board Members*
      1. To meet annually to discuss policies and procedures governing the home.

2.   To receive updates and reports on new and former residents.
3.   To discuss new vision and new direction for the home.
4.   To provide accountability to the director and the house staff.
5.   To discuss and implement financial strategies for the home as approved by the president.
6.   To review yearly budgets and expenses.
7.   To assist in fund-raising for the program's operation and growth.

II.   **House Staff Qualifications**
A.   *Director*
1.   Be a person of vision.
2.   Be a person full of compassion.
3.   Be a person of integrity and character.
4.   Be teachable.
5.   Have managerial and administrative skills.

B.   *House Parents*
1.   Be a person of vision.
2.   Be qualified on the basis of personal character to work with women in crisis.
3.   Be capable of providing leadership and spiritual guidance to each of the women according to her specific needs.
4.   Be capable of providing structure, love, and discipleship to women in crisis.
5.   Be compassionate and be able to give love to women in a crisis situation.
6.   Be qualified by having personal parenting skills and experience with children.
7.   Be qualified with managerial and administration skills.
8.   Be able to teach and be teachable.
9.   Be a person of integrity and character and be willing to lead the women by example.

C.   *Advocates*
An advocate is one who stands in the gap for another in need. All advocates should be approved by the president, the director and the house parents.
1.   Be willing to be used according to their abilities and the needs of the home.
2.   Be an active member of their local churches.

123

3. Have the heart of a servant and reflect the character and nature of Jesus.

4. Complete an application and have an interview with the house parent.

5. Instruct a woman in any decision, or counsel any woman only with the house parents' permission or direction.

6. Be dedicated to the mission of the program.

7. Display compassion for the women.

8. Be interested in every woman's well-being and success.

9. Be committed to the vision, and to the success of the program.

10. Be a team player.

11. Have talents which can benefit the program.

III. Financial Responsibility

A. *General Requirements*

1. The president shall determine and review annually the cost of care, defining the various items to be included.

2. Receipts shall be secured for all payments and for all monies received by the home.

3. The home shall carry liability insurance.

B. *Budget Provisions*

1. Salaries

2. Cost of food and supplies

3. Cost of mortgage

4. Adequate transportation and maintenance

5. Adequate physical facilities, equipment and maintenance

6. Insurance and taxes

C. *Funding the Operation*

1. Annual Givers. Annual givers are the backbone of the home. It is a goal to have annual givers as the means of support for the life of the home.

2. Fund-raisers. Fund-raisers provide cash flow in the home. This form of contribution allows the residents to get involved and take ownership of the house. Creativity and the right product can produce needed money for the home.

3. Banquets. Holding banquets is another way to bring all of the community resources together to share success and vision. It also opens the door to invite potential business and community contacts into your crisis home.

4. In-kind Donations. In-kind donations provide a way to obtain the necessary material you need to maintain your home. In-kind donations can come from retail stores, markets, homes, and drives (toys, hygiene, and clothes, etc.)
5. Resident Support Letter. Each resident, upon her arrival, writes a letter to her family, church, friends, and other supporters. She explains why she is participating in the program and her need for financial support. A cover letter written by the director is placed with the resident's letter and sent to all of the resident's outside supporters.

THE PROGRAM'S RESOURCES

A. **General Services**
1. Christ-centered counseling by the pastor or staff ministers is available at any time, at the request of the women or staff when deemed necessary.
2. Career counseling is available. Women will be accompanied on job interviews and related appointments.
3. Recreational outings and activities are planned for women, as they are physically able to participate.
4. Women are guided in choosing a school for educational purposes. Women have the opportunity to pursue GED while in the home.
5. All pregnant women will attend childbirth/parenting education classes taught by qualified staff.
6. At the women's request, outside adoption services are available.
7. Women are given teaching on budgeting and finances.
8. Upon completion of the Hiding Place program and the "Buds to Roses" life skills curriculum, a woman will be considered for graduation.
9. A woman is eligible to receive a scholarship upon graduation from the Hiding Place program. If a woman leaves the program early and does not complete assignments, she forfeits her scholarship eligibility opportunity.

B. **The Hiding Place provides:**
1. A Christ-centered family life setting
2. Love to hurting women
3. Personal life skills training
4. Personal hygiene development
5. Discipline
6. Healing
7. Medical exams

8. Pre- and post-natal care
9. Spiritual growth—every woman is strengthened through help from the pastor, devotions, godly staff and volunteers, prayer, local church support, and church attendance.

COMMUNITY RESOURCES

A. **The Department of Social Services (DSS)**
DSS has many resources that can assist your women's work. The following services are available:
1. TCA—Temporary case assistance
2. Food stamps
3. Family services
4. Job networking
5. Daycare vouchers
6. Medical assistance
7. WIC
8. Homeless network

All of these services are available to the residences in any community. The key is using these services temporarily and not permanently. Social workers have been very helpful in giving information and insight into how these programs work. Making friends in the DSS has proven to be very helpful and useful to our women's work.

B. **Schools**
Schools have also proven to be a great resource. The schools have used this home to educate students on crisis pregnancy and homelessness. Schools look for community services opportunities for students. During the holiday season, area schools that have developed a partnership with the Hiding Place give donations, including much-needed hygiene items and clothing.

C. **Hospitals**
Locating a hospital is crucial to a successful work. Make an appointment with the director of the hospital and explain the program. Once the presentation is made and all parties have agreed to work together, nurture the relationship with visits from time to time. Once a relationship is established, it opens many other doors of opportunity, such as pediatric care for the babies and classes for new moms. Hospitals are great resources of information and support.

D. **Transitional Programs**
Transitional programs in your area are great resources for a women's work. Once a woman completes the Hiding Place program, she is eligible to move into a transitional program or a welfare-to-work program. The government sets up many of these programs. They offer

job training, on-site daycare, and semi-independent living. These programs are listed with the Department of Social Services. Partnering with these programs is beneficial, especially when a woman has no other family support.

E.   **Networking**

Networking is an important key to having a successful home. Connecting with people and building relationships make the program take on an inviting atmosphere to outsiders. Connecting with community outreaches strengthens the work and allows you to have options and answers for women in crisis as well as their family and friends. Networking gives you more resources to meet the needs of the women.

F.   **Crisis Pregnancy Centers**

Crisis Pregnancy Centers are an excellent source for making the home known. Send a simple letter outlining the program, along with a brochure and name of a contact person. This opens a way for women to learn about the program. Word-of-mouth, schools, hospitals, and juvenile programs are also ways of making the program known.

Appendix B

Nehemiah House

The following section is a simple layout of how to start and establish a men's shelter and program in your area. By utilizing some of these basic rules, you can begin to plan a program in your area to aid those who are homeless and suffering from addictions. The outline is not a total picture of what you can do to make this type of program happen in your area. However, it is a great starting point!

FINANCING A MEN'S SHELTER

Three people within your local government are keys in establishing a homeless shelter. A good working relationship with these key people is essential. Spend some quality time with these officials, and build good communication with them.

A. **Community Development Director or Coordinator**

This person is the one to whom your vision or idea must be sold. He or she then will ultimately have to sell the idea to the mayor, county executive and community. This individual is responsible to coordinate the entire operation if you plan to work in conjunction with the government in your local jurisdiction.

B. **Grant Administration Office**

This is the office where the grants issued by your local government will be officiated. They will help you in filling out the paperwork, communicating deadlines for reports, and informing you about upcoming grants for which your program may be qualified.

C. **Homeless Service Coordinator**

This individual has current information on all the homeless issue(s) in your area. He or she is usually open to new ideas for eliminating homelessness. The homeless service coordinator will be vital for input, resources, and program development. Because of experience with many other programs, the coordinator can offer quality advice on what you care to do. The homeless service coordinator can give particular assistance when you are developing a service program that will pass Housing and Urban Development (HUD) guidelines.

How to proceed in working with the local government:

1. Determine if there is a need to help the homeless in your area.
2. Submit the program idea to the three key people in your jurisdiction.
3. Research, design, and submit grant applications to organizations for funding.
4. Contact HUD about their guidelines if you plan to receive funding from them.
5. Find out if your grants were approved.
6. Find out if the local jurisdiction is going to supply funding.
7. Begin the process of construction and operation of the program.

STARTING A NEHEMIAH HOUSE PROGRAM

Use the following guidelines to determine whether to open a homeless program.

- Is there really a need for a homeless program in your area?
- Research existing programs already being funded by the county, state, federal governments, and private foundations in your area.
    1. Are existing programs meeting the homeless need?
    2. Are existing programs draining the county and state?
    3. Are the county and state looking for another approach to this need?
    4. If they are not open to this program, you must sell them on the idea.
- Do you have an individual (champion) to run the program who is:
    1. Compassionate (it's best if they have experienced homelessness themselves)
    2. Familiar with drug and alcohol abuse
    3. Qualified counselor
    4. Skilled in management and administration
    5. Responsible steward of all duties
    6. Patient and easygoing

- Gather statistics and facts such as actual testimonies of change in individuals within the community. Check statistical sections in the humanities and social science areas of your local library for help with this.
    1. Example: In Baltimore County there was a 92 percent increase in homelessness between 1995 and 1996.
    2. Example: Of all the homeless people in Baltimore County, 48 percent are male, 52 percent are women with children.
- Find a suitable location for a shelter with proper zoning to build and operate.
- Develop a program from start to finish. See yourself as the owner, manager, and staff person. Determine what it will take to operate and make this a pattern program to assist the people you wish to help.
- Submit vision and program to the community development director for approval.
- Gain non-profit status and incorporate the program or shelter.
- Appoint an executive board.
- Pursue funding through grants and donations.
- Establish a qualified bookkeeping/accounting department that can manage grant funding (records and disbursement).
- Build and operate the shelter/program.

NEHEMIAH HOUSE SERVICE PLANS

For any resident who wants to enter Phase II, Phase III or the Protective Care Program, compliance to the service plan is essential. The service plan assists the resident in becoming self-sufficient and independent from the cycles that have affected his life. Every resident will fill out a standard questionnaire and agree to the standard rules of the shelter at intake. However, for the man who wants to further his life, the agreement to the service plan will depend on his willingness to continue on with the other phases. If the resident does not wish to continue, he will be limited to a 14-day stay in Phase I.

The Nehemiah House exists for two purposes. The first is to provide temporary but necessary shelter, food, clothing, and physical care for homeless men. The second is to provide a program to help men eliminate their homeless situation by making them responsible to themselves and their families while becoming useful members of the community and society.

To address the homeless problem in Baltimore County, Nehemiah House, Inc. has been providing, since January 23, 1991, the first year-round shelter and rehabilitation program for males in this community. We continue to provide and maintain a quality program characterized by flexibility and a high degree of professionalism. The program is designed with a three-phase concept. Phases I and II are for emergency housing, whereas Phase III is transitional. Also, within the operations of our service plan, we have a program, called the Protective Care Plan, to assist those suffering from addictions.

The following are examples of the service plans that we use to assist our residents.

Phase I–Observation Phase

> The induction phase will provide basic life-sustaining care (food and lodging) for the homeless individual in a dormitory-type setting for a maximum of 21 days. This is the observation phase to determine entry into Phase II.

Phase II–Adjustment Phase

> After successful completion of Phase I, the homeless individual moves into the next phase. During Phase II, the resident and the caseworker draft and agree to a service plan that addresses the development, maintenance, or furtherance of basic life skills and the elimination of dependency. The plan is reviewed and revised as necessary by staff, the resident, and the caseworker. Goals are established and progress is monitored jointly by Nehemiah House staff and the homeless individual. Maximum stay in this phase is ten additional weeks.

Service plan goals may include but are not limited to the following:

- furtherance of education
- seeking vocational training/job opportunities
- individual or group counseling
- obtaining legal entitlement such as pension benefits
- assistance with acquiring disability benefits
- placement in substance abuse programs (both inpatient and outpatient)

Phase III–Discipleship and Transitional Housing

> Phase III is unlike phases I and II. At entry into phase III, a new service plan and new goals will be established which will take the individual towards self-sufficiency and re-entry into society. The phase III individual is, to an ever-increasing degree, participating on his own initiative in activities which promote and characterize responsible behavior to himself, his family and the community, while he pursues personal goals and obligations. This plan offers a Christ-centered opportunity for the resident to increase his faith. Maximum stay is three months.

Protective Care Discipleship Program

> Any resident who enters our facility and wishes to receive help for addictions to drug and alcohol may enter this program. It is a three-month program where the resident is required to remain at the

facility. Many residents who come to us are looking for help beyond Alcoholics/Narcotics Anonymous. This plan assists men with help according to biblical and moral principles of:

- faith in the Lord Jesus Christ
- prayer and Bible studies
- rebuilding relationships with families
- community service work (requirement—six hours per day, four or five days per week)
- recreation (at local parks, gymnasiums, the facility, etc.)
- day trips (camping, hiking, museums, cookouts, community picnics, etc.)
- medical assistance (through local hospitals, social services, private practitioners, etc.)

After completing this three-month program the resident is given the opportunity to continue into Phase III. The Protective Care Discipleship Program, in conjunction with the standard operation of our other phases, has assisted the addict with his life-controlling issue.

Appendix C

A Can Can Make a Difference (CCMAD)

- A Can Can Make a Difference (CCMAD) is a community-based program comprised of churches, grocery stores, businesses/corporations, food pantries/soup kitchens, community associations, government agencies, and institutions working together to feed the hungry of Baltimore City, surrounding counties and the State of Maryland.
- The goal of CCMAD is to accumulate a large volume of both perishable and non-perishable food items. This resource of food is then distributed as swiftly and efficiently as possible to every legitimate non-profit food distribution agency.
- This program is designed to be effectively implemented for both a small-scale operation as well as a city and/or statewide—even national scale.
- *There is absolutely no fee or charge for food items distributed by A Can Can Make a Difference.* All food items received by this program are distributed to associated food distribution agencies without cost. Food donated or freely given by individuals and companies should not and will not then be sold to those distributing it to the hungry. This is a tenet requiring strict adherence by those participating in this program.

- *Hunger can be defeated–this is a winnable war!* The goal and commitment of A Can Can Make a Difference is to totally eradicate hunger from our communities, city and state. It is not designed to "lessen the problem," "take care of some," or to "make more palatable the statistics." This program's purpose is to eliminate the plight of the hungry as we know it today.

I. **Promotion**

   A. Identify a local celebrity or dignitary to be a spokesperson for the CCMAD program. Use them for official statements, television spots and store appearances.

   B. Produce other promotional pieces, such as posters, magnetic signs for delivery trucks, a promotional video and CCMAD letterhead.

II. **Participation, Contribution, and Sponsorship**

   Print contribution cards and distribute them to participating stores and churches. It is important that the CCMAD program be under a corporation with a tax-exempt, non-profit status so contributors may receive tax credit.

   Soliciting contributions and sponsorship

   - Contact area grocery stores by letter; follow up with a phone call and arrange a personal meeting with the manager.
   - At the meeting, leave a letter and any other literature with him/her.
   - Promote the point of increased sales to the store, as well as doing their part to end hunger.
   - Contact local churches by phone call and letter.
   - Get a contact name.
   - Upon their agreement to participate in the program, send the contact a follow-up letter with all the particulars as well as art work for their bulletin flyers.
   - Contact local soup kitchens, food pantries, halfway houses and food distribution centers, informing them of the program.
   - Get contact names, and keep a list of those who desire to participate.
   - Contact local television, radio, newspapers and other media for sponsorships and coverage.

III. **Distribution and Storage**

   A. *The warehouse*

   The warehouse facility must have adequate unloading, packing and storage space. The warehouse needs an individual assigned as a supervisor, plus volunteers to unload, sort, box, stamp, count, weigh, and load cans. Volunteers can come from participating churches, colleges, food agencies and local community service organizations. Court-assigned workers can be found in the work-release prison programs.

B. *Super Pantries*

"Super Pantries" can be established in specific and strategic locations within a community. They function like the main warehouse but on a smaller scale. For example, a city could be divided into four districts with a super pantry in each district. The super pantries supply all the distributors from their own warehouse within their prescribed boundaries.

C. *State Distribution Centers*

Distribution centers should be set up across the state, and managed by pastors assigned to be the "food distributors" in their areas. Their responsibilities include ordering and receiving shipments of food from the headquarters warehouse. They advertise, develop relationships with and distribute food items to local churches, food pantries, soup kitchens, etc. in the program area. Through the state distribution centers this program can move from a city to a state level. An important stipulation upon the state distributors is that there can be absolutely no stockpiling. Goods must be moved as soon as possible.

D. *Shipping*

1. Send letters to area truck rental and fuel companies. Make follow-up appointments to request this type of sponsorship.

2. Post a map of the area the program is serving, with the warehouse (main storage facility) and the participating stores, etc. identified and labeled. From this you will ascertain:
   - a travel route from store to store for pick-up
   - estimated time involved
   - what size truck is needed
   - estimated daily/weekly fuel consumption

3. Arrange a schedule of qualified drivers and helpers, giving the time of day and route plan. Be sure to have an alternate person in case someone has to cancel. Give the drivers a precise, clear route with directions to the warehouse and stores.

NOTE: Insurance may be needed to cover trucks.

E. *Receptacles*

Chemical companies or packaging businesses may provide drums for a donation or a nominal cost. Drums with a capacity of 55 pounds or more work well. Paint and label the drums, and deliver these to participating locations. Also provide a poster with a brief, eye-catching statement about the program to be placed above the receptacle.

IV. **Three Major Groups of CCMAD**

    A. *Churches*

    He who has pity on the poor lends to the Lord (Proverbs 19:17a).

    [Jesus said] *"I was hungry and you gave Me food; I was thirsty and you gave Me drink"* (Matthew 25:35a).

It is the commission of the Church to feed the hungry and preach the gospel to the poor. The Church is absolutely vital to the success of this program and should be the very foundation of its structure. There are several points to consider:

- All churches will acknowledge the duty to feed the hungry.
- This duty is non-controversial and non-threatening, transcending denominational and sectarian walls.
- The churches of our community and city will unite in this effort, thus creating a powerful force of resources.
- Through the organization of the Church, both locally and in a wider-based area, tens of thousands of individuals can be mobilized for the cause.

    1. How a church can actively participate in the program

- Most churches are aware of the need to feed the hungry and to have some type of program, i.e., a "helps" or a "food pantry" ministry. This program can be helpful to either inspire a church to begin a food pantry or to enlarge their vision to the city if one is already established. Most churches that do feed the hungry and have food pantries do not have enough food, and are looking for additional sources of supply.
- It is very important when making contact with a pastor or church leader not to ask them to join "your program." Emphasize individual management/ownership/partnership to all participants. The best results will take place when a pastor is informed of how his church can be a part of a program that will both supply food and give creative ways to raise food items.
- One individual should take the responsibility of being a pastor/church representative to maintain relations with those participating. As the program grows, it may be necessary to divide participating pastors into groups, each group having its own representative.

- Write a letter to area pastors.
- Send the first letter to churches with a relationship already established.
- Next, send letters to churches in close proximity to participating stores.
- Follow up with a phone call. Record all information on a church follow-up form.
- Be prepared to send a CCMAD representative if pastors request a speaker to address their committees, etc. This could prove very beneficial in establishing inter-community church relationships.

2. Key points to communicate to these pastors/church leaders:
   - From the pulpit, the pastor can share and exhort the congregation to participate.
   - The church can distribute flyers with the Sunday bulletin. (Included in your mail-out to these participating churches, should be an "original" flyer that they can copy many times and have it remain presentable.)
   - Communicate the importance of each church getting volunteers to work at the warehouse or to distribute flyers in grocery stores.
   - Send them monthly reports giving the latest program developments, number of cans of food collected, etc.
   - *Stay in dialogue with the participants!*
   - Schedule a meeting for participating leaders in every locale to discuss the program and get answers to their questions.

B. *Stores*
   - Stores are a very essential part of the CCMAD program simply because this is where the food is. As a general rule, most grocery stores are looking to participate in a program that is effectively and sincerely feeding the hungry. Upon this premise, it is with confidence that store owners and managers can be approached about their support of the program.
   - The store officials we have worked with have volunteered to purchase stampers, tape and tape dispensers, boxes, crates, as well as to finance the printing of materials, etc.
   - It is very important to assign a CCMAD representative to maintain both an oversight of the store's participation as well as to establish a working relationship with the managers. As stores are added, as in the case with pastors, it

may be beneficial to divide an area into zones, appointing zone supervisors.

1.   Enlisting store participation in the CCMAD program:
- Contact a store your church has already established a relationship with, or a store located near your church, or a store known for its community service.
- Write a brief, professional letter to the store manager.
- Follow up with a phone call to request an appointment at the manager's convenience.

2.   Store participation
- Managers place signs or posters in front windows or doors.
- Cashiers wear CCMAD buttons.
- Cashiers place flyers or contribution cards in shoppers' bags.
- Posters in the canned food aisles remind shoppers to contribute.
- Managers make announcements over the public address system—"Don't forget your can..."

C.   *Distributors*

Distributors are all groups or agencies who receive food from the CCMAD program. These groups include churches, soup kitchens, food pantries, shelters, halfway houses, and community associations. Such agencies can be identified and verified through:
- Department of Human Resources
- Mayor's or governor's office
- State Food Committee
- Department of Social Services

1.   Requirements for distributors
- Distributors will not be responsible to deliver food to individuals and families. Nor will the CCMAD warehouse do food transactions with individuals, but only with distribution agencies. The concept is for the warehouse to supply to the food agencies, who then give to the individuals and to families. Requests by individuals or families will be referred to affiliate agencies and CCMAD will make sure their need is met.
- There must be absolutely no stockpiling of food. As the main warehouse receives and moves food as quickly as possible, so must food pantries, churches and soup kitchens. If the main warehouse is made aware that a

group is stockpiling food, an immediate call will be made to rectify the situation.

- Food items are given to distributors from CCMAD absolutely free of charge. Distributors will not sell food items to individuals or any other group. All cans are stamped "Not for Resale"—"Freely you have received, freely you shall give."

- A distributor must register with CCMAD and receive a non-transferable distributor's card. Pertinent information is filled out on the card which is signed and a photo I.D. is put on the reverse side. All food transactions are made through this card. Without a personal, signed card, the distributor may not receive or pick up food.

- Upon receipt of food, the distributor card is punched at the appropriate date.

- If more than one representative from a food distributing agency will be picking up food orders, each one will need his or her own distributor's card.

2. Ordering food items

- A CCMAD phone line must be established and given out to all participants. This line can be located at the main office (church, business) or the warehouse. As well and if possible, a fax machine is very efficient. Orders could be faxed 24 hours a day. It is also advisable to have an answering machine to take messages after hours. It is to your advantage to respond to every call as soon as possible.

- Distributors should pick up food from the warehouse. As a standard policy, allow one working day's time to sort, inspect, stamp, pack and prepare orders.

- Use standard food order forms to help expedite the entire ordering, packing, and shipping process.

Appendix D

Adopt-A-Block

PHASE I—Planning/Preparing for the Block Party

I. **Logistics**
  A. *Select a time and date for a block party*
      1. The best time is when most people in the neighborhood are home and available.
      2. Try not to schedule the party during another church or community event.
      3. Establish communication with the local police department and community association and inquire for a date and time that works well with them.
  B. *Select a location*
      1. Pray! This is the most important tool; God has a predetermined location.
      2. Work closely with the police, since they will be blocking off the roads and patrolling the event.
          a. The police department will offer statistics concerning high drug and crime areas.
          b. The police department is aware of the level of resident involvement with law enforcement—for example, which neighborhoods have crime watch programs.

3. Select a block near other local churches; they offer potential assistance and resources.
4. Look for available vacant houses
   a. This is very important and is one of the prime considerations for selecting a block.
   b. Vacant houses are potential houses to renovate and set up Adopt-A-Block headquarters or family residences (an essential ingredient in the block adoption process).

C. *Secure the location*
   1. Contact the local community association
      a. This is very important! This local community group is comprised of some of the residents of the block. Take care not to offend or overlook this group, but to work with them closely from the outset.
      b. Identify the community leader and develop a working relationship.
      c. It is important to allow the community association opportunity for expression during the event.

D. *File for permits*
   1. Go in person, meet an individual you can make a personal contact with, and share the vision.
      a. Barricade permit (normal fee).
      b. Gathering permit (normal fee).
      c. Food permit (since you are a non-profit group, this should be gratis).

E. *Obtain stages, booths and tables*
   1. The city should supply these, usually through the mayor's Special Events office.
   2. If given proper time and notice (the more time the better), the city will usually deliver, set up and remove these items.
   3. Application fee and deposit may be required. Request the city's waiving of all fees and deposits due to the non-profit, pro-community nature of the event.

F. *Arrange for trash removal*
   1. The city should supply trash cans and a dumpster. Work through the sanitation department.
   2. Establish a clean-up crew to remove all the trash and debris after the block party. Make it a priority to leave the block cleaner than you found it.

G. *Locate bathroom facilities*
   1. Check with portable toilet companies for two units for the day. Inquire about having them donated.
   2. If this is not possible, the city may have these facilities—or ask a community resident or church for use of their facility for party volunteers.

H. *Arrange for electricity*
   1. The local power company will usually allow use from a nearby power company pole (the charge for temporary service could be several hundred dollars).
   2. Check with private homeowners or a church for access to electricity.
   3. It is wise to have several generators on hand for emergency power.

II. Dignitaries and Community Services
Contact and involve the following:
A. Police department
B. Fire department
C. Professional athletes
D. Government officials
E. Community agencies and services
   1. Health screening by area hospitals
   2. Drug and substance abuse
   3. Alcoholics and Narcotics Anonymous
   4. Housing Authority. This department of the city is invaluable because of its access to pertinent information such as zoning, availability of houses, names of owners and landlords, health violations, taxes and liens, urban development programs, and so on.
   5. Education programs. This is essential and can include both private and public programs. The public school system has many programs available for various situations and age groups. Private programs such as "Sing, Spell, Learn" and G.E.D. classes are beneficial.
   6. Job placement agencies. There are many government and private employment agencies and counseling services available. Look for the groups that are willing to work with the same sacrificial commitment to the residents as Adopt-A-Block does. This is an important area.
   7. Senior care

8. Pro-life programs
9. Red Cross. With ample notification, the Red Cross will send out their units and team to serve the people at the block party.

III. Pastors and Local Churches

A. By letter, telephone, then a personal visit, contact pastors of local churches within a one- to five-mile radius of the adopted block.

B. Contact all churches that are already in a working relationship with your church or group.

C. Share the vision and develop a core of committed, working pastors and churches.
1. Have a special breakfast or luncheon and share Adopt-A-Block.
2. Show the video and give out literature.
3. Invite pastors to the actual block party.

D. Suggest ways for pastors and congregations to get involved.
1. Participate in prayer rallies.
2. Contribute audio and video equipment.
3. Supply altar workers.
4. Follow up with new converts.
5. Contribute resources such as clothes, groceries, Bibles, toys, food, etc.
6. Provide singers, musicians, clowns, puppets.
7. Volunteer for setup and cleanup crews.
8. Canvass the neighborhood and distribute flyers.
9. Sponsor or help at booths.
10. Contribute finances.

E. Involve as many pastors as possible, in order to gain the most contacts with businessmen, contractors, and community and government officials.

IV. Business Sponsorships and Contributions

This is a very important ingredient in the success of the Adopt-A-Block program. Participation of private business is important because it generates revenue and resources, and gives businesses the opportunity to be involved in their communities. The goal is to solicit companies in the city to enter into the sponsorship program.

A. Contact local businesses with a letter and personal call requesting donations for the block party.
1. If possible, make an appointment and visit personally.

    2.   The goal is for the private business sector to supply the funds and resources for the block party.

B.   Explain Adopt-A-Block sponsorship programs

    1.   Annual sponsor—sponsor who donates goods, services, or finances to cover the needs of one year of block parties and ongoing block events (probably four events per year, plus occasional dinners and special needs).

    2.   Single event sponsor—sponsor who donates goods, services, or finances for a single defined block party event or specific purpose or need.

    3.   General contributor—company or individual who cannot donate goods or services to support a block party, but who wants to be a part of the giving by providing either financial support or goods to be managed by Adopt-A-Block wherever the need exists in the city.

These items can be used for ongoing block support in the neighborhoods after the initial block party is finished and we adopt the block.

PHASE II—Invasion/The Block Party

I.   **Prayer**

A.   This is a crucial area. Take special care not to neglect or overlook this. Remember, the battle is won in the air through prayer and intercession; the spoils of victory are taken through obedient service.

B.   Set up nightly prayer rallies for the two weeks prior to the block party.

C.   Encourage participating churches to hold special prayer and intercession times.

D.   Hold a large prayer rally with all participating parties at the block party site the night before the event.

E.   Sponsoring churches can use their own creativity in planning prayer for their block parties. Again, the importance of covering this program with prayer cannot be overemphasized. You are entering into satan's strongholds!

II.   **Schedule or Order of Events**

A.   Block party could run three to four hours, beginning 12:00 noon on a Saturday.

B.   Allow three to four hours' transportation and setup time prior to opening the event.

C. *Very important!* Communicate with the residents of the block and work with the police department to ensure that residents move their vehicles off the street. The night before is the best time to do this.

D. Plan an agenda of activities.

III. Booths

The city should have booths available, which they will set up. If not, booths can be constructed by volunteers.

Booth suggestions:

A. Clothing

B. Groceries

C. Concession stand

D. Drug and substance abuse

E. Medical/health screenings

F. Pro-life

G. Bibles and tracts

H. Health services

I. Senior care

J. Children's

K. Educational booth

L. Employment

M. Community association booth—the association may want a booth for public relations promotion or to pass out literature. It is important to always offer this booth to the association.

N. Local churches—some churches may desire booths to pass out church literature, calendars of events, etc. It is wise to have a set policy that nothing is to be sold at the block party. The spirit of the event is to give and serve.

O. Adopt-A-Block booth—This booth can be the nerve center for information and for paging people. The booth may have a sign-in sheet for pastors and community officials.

Important: All booths and related activities (including the grill) shut down for the closing ministry. Everyone is encouraged to move toward the stage.

IV. Altar Workers

A. Before the event, train and prepare counselors to minister to people responding to the closing altar call.

B. Record the name and pertinent information of the new converts on a "new convert" or "decision" slip.

   C.   A three-part new convert slip is very effective, because the information is then available to the altar worker, the pastor or the follow-up church, and the follow-up supervisor.

   D.   Encourage altar workers to make contact with the individuals they counseled and seek to disciple them.

   E.   Altar workers should come from all participating churches.

V.   **Ministry**

   A.   Altar workers witness and hand out tracts during the block party.

   B.   Ministers provide exhortation and prayer throughout the block party.

   C.   Closing ministry

       1.   Music ministry.

       2.   All booth activities stop. Call everyone to move to stage. A pastor speaks (either the sponsoring pastor or the pastor of the closest church).

       3.   Give an altar call for salvation, healing, deliverance, etc.

       4.   Pastors and altar workers pray with and get names of the people.

       5.   It is effective to close the event with all the pastors and community leaders gathered on the stage, holding hands and praying for God's blessing over the block.

       6.   Encourage the people that transportation will be provided to get them to church Sunday morning.

       7.   New converts who have exceptional testimonies may share at this time.

PHASE III—OCCUPATION/ADOPTING THE BLOCK

This phase of the program is as important as the previous two. No matter how successful the block party itself may have been, it is ultimately the follow-up program that reveals the fruit of the event and whether or not a true "adoption" has taken place.

I.   **Follow-up**

   A.   Encourage altar workers or pastors to follow up with new converts on the same day that the block party was held. They can offer a word of encouragement and an invitation to church Sunday morning.

   B.   Conduct a survey.

   C.   Meet immediate needs.

D.   Establish block captain(s)—find the resident(s) who is/are the neighborhood spokesperson or activist and work closely with them as a liaison between Adopt-A-Block and the people.

The objective of follow-up is to develop a trust with the people and lead them step-by-step into a place of self-help and restored pride and motivation. The goal is to include residents of an Adopt-A-Block in the work to adopt the next block.

The daily and weekly presence of pastors and Adopt-A-Block leaders in the adopted block builds more and more trust with the people and sends a strong signal to drug dealers that their presence will not be tolerated.

II.   Possess a house(s) on each adopted block.

A.   Identify each vacant home on the block and find out who owns each one. The police department or city housing authority can access this information.

B.   Determine the zoning and in all dialogue emphasize renovating houses for resident dwellings as opposed to religious activities.

C.   We strongly suggest that you meet with the highest echelon figure in the city bureaucracy in this matter. A friend in this area of affairs is invaluable. Without establishing relationship with an individual, you will inevitably get caught up in the bureaucratic maze.

D.   If a house is city-owned, ask the city to donate it and waive any lien or taxes. If the house is privately owned—write a letter, call, and if necessary, personally visit the individual. Ask the owner to donate the house for a tax credit.

If the house is privately owned and has been vacant for some time, chances are good it has been condemned or cited by the health department. This can be checked through the health department.

E.   Houses may be secured at a minimal cost if the proper negotiations are made.

F.   Participating contractors, neighborhood residents, and congregational tradesman can work together to renovate the house.

G.   Check with the housing authority and urban development group for potential city, state, or federal grants to help purchase or renovate a house.

H.   Upon renovation, move into the house a committed, trained, strong Christian family. The family will oversee Adopt-A-Block activities for that block and "pastor" the people of the block.

This family is, in effect, an extension of the ministry of Adopt-A-Block or a local pastor.

I.   The house and its family can be a center for:
1.   Counseling
2.   Contact point for community agencies
3.   Prayer meetings or Bible studies
4.   G.E.D
5.   Boy Scouts or youth programs

J.   To effectively adopt a block, it is essential to purchase houses and place strong Christian families in that block.

Appendix E

Grant Writing

STEPS TO DEVELOPING YOUR PROGRAM

A. **Learn the needs of your local community**
1. Contact the local department of social services, the governor's or mayor's office and local social programs.
   Ask them for any contracts, statistics or annual reports based on the need which you desire to address. (Example: If you are interested in adolescent pregnancy, contact the governor's office and request their report on your state's history of the need, as well as the name of a resource person who can help you.)
2. These individuals and reports will tell you where the gaps for services are in your communities, and will also give you vital information to put in your grant.
3. If you can fill the gap with your program and have it line up with what the foundation's funding interests are, you have a good hook to open the eyes of a foundation to read your proposal.

B. **Write your vision and make it plain**
1. Before beginning to write grant proposals, make sure you have a well-developed business plan for your program.

2. Establish the program concept, the mission statement, the kind of people you want to help, guidelines, needs, etc.

3. Think of yourself as the owner, director, and recipient of the program. What will you need to make your program become a reality and be successful?

4. Use a planning guide to help you brainstorm grant ideas.

C. **Learning How to Write Grants**

1. Take a course at:

> The Foundation Center
> 1001 Connecticut Avenue, NW
> Washington, DC 20036
> Phone (202) 331-1400
> WEBSITE: www.fdncenter.org
> (They offer satellite courses in most states)

2. Read *The Foundation Center's Guide to Proposal Writing* by Jane Geever & Patricia McNeill.

3. Take the "First Course in Fundraising"—a two day, entry-level fund-raising course sponsored by:

> National Society of Fundraising Executives (NSFRE)
> King Street, Suite 700
> Alexandria, VA 22314
> Phone (703) 684-0410 or 1-800-688-FIND
> WEBSITE: www.nsfre.org
> (There is a chapter in almost every state)

D. **Local places of reference to begin your grant research**

1. Visit your local library and request resources on grant writing, proposal writing, fund-raising or philanthropy. Most libraries carry Foundation Center books. Ask them if they have a Foundation Center Cooperating Collection on-site. These are some of the most requested books for foundation information.

2. Visit the Foundation Center or check out their website.

E. **Make sure that**

1. You are incorporated

2. You have by-laws, officers, a board of directors

3. You are a 501(c)3 tax-exempt charitable organization

Note: *Most* foundations and corporate philanthropy do not support organizations where these components are not in place. It is much easier to complete these steps with the help of an attorney, accountant, etc.

F. **Have appropriate audit reports or good financial proof of your current spending activities.**

1. Foundations want to know what you are doing with the money you already have. Are you being a good steward?
2. Foundations won't give you their money if you are not being responsible and have no legitimate proof.
3. If this is a new program concept, have a financial plan and budget developed. Advise the organization that at the end of your first fiscal year you will be doing an audit of any funds which are received as contributions.

G. Guidelines of the foundations
1. Foundations are sticklers for accuracy in filing applications or submitting proposals.
2. As you research you will see that many foundations have particular interests. Find the ones that line up with your program plans.
3. Contact them and ask for their guidelines.
4. Make sure you have a good idea of what you want to do. They may ask questions about your program and why you are writing to them or want their guidelines.

H. Getting funding from the government
Ask your local government grants administration office (in the social or human services department of your area), the Federal Register, or the Foundation Center for information on any government grants that may apply to your proposed plan/program. Some of the more common grant names are:
- FEMA–Federal Emergency Management Assistance
- CDBG–Community Development Block Grants
- ESG/McKinney–Emergency Shelter Grants
- Emergency Shelter Fund
- HUD–Housing and Urban Development
- HOPWA–Housing for Persons with AIDS
- Family Violence and Prevention Services Grants

HOW TO RESEARCH FOUNDATIONS

How do I determine who will fund my projects? When doing research, break down your project based on these areas: Subject (*what?*), Geography (*where?*), Demographics (*who are the recipients?*), Is There a Need (*why?*), Your Timeline (*when?*).

POSSIBLE FOUNDATION FUNDING SOURCES

A. Subject Search
Purpose: to match your project idea with a foundation. What do they like?
(the homeless, children, etc.)

Examine the indexes of Foundation Center grant books
- in Foundation Directory
- in Foundation/Corporation Annual Reports
- in foundations' IRS tax returns and 990s

Examine subject indexes
- in Foundation Directory
- Source Book Profiles

B. Geographic Search:
Purpose: To locate a foundation source in a specific region.
1. Smaller grants or local projects.
2. Use grant books arranged by state or geographic index. See which ones in your state/area will support your efforts.

QUESTIONS TO ASK A FOUNDATION

1. Has the foundation funded several projects in your field?
2. Does the foundation make grants in your geographic location?
3. Does the foundation make grants in the size you are requesting?
4. Does the foundation make grants for operating budgets, building, equipment, capital projects, etc.?
5. Will the foundation fully fund a project or do they prefer sharing or matching funding?
6. For what time period does the foundation make grants? (one time/continuing support)
7. What types of organizations does the foundation support?
8. Are there application deadlines?
9. Do they want a full proposal or just a letter of intent in the beginning?
10. What is their median giving for the foundation?

Always research a foundation before you send a proposal. Your chances of receiving a grant will be greater if you take the time to introduce yourself and your agency before filing an application.

Grant resources to get you started
The Foundation Center
Connecticut Avenue NW
Suite 938
Washington DC 20036
PH #: 202-331-1400
Internet: http://www.fdncenter.org
Purpose: Library of Foundations and Philanthropy
National Society of Fundraising Executives (NSFRE)

NSFRE Foundation
King Street, Suite 700
Alexandria, VA 22314
PH#: 703-684-0410 or 1-800-666-3863
Internet: www.nsfre.org
Purpose: Resource on all levels of giving, fund-raising and volunteerism.

Chronicle of Philanthropy
P.O. Box 1989
Marion, OH 43306-2089
Internet: http://philanthropy.com
Purpose: Magazine of Philanthropy and Grant Writing

BOOKS
- *National Directory of Corporate Giving*—The Foundation Center
- *The Foundation Directory*—The Foundation Center
- *National Guide to Funding in Religion*—The Foundation Center
- *Born to Raise*—Jerold Panas
- *Achieving Excellence in Fund Raising*—Henry A. Rosso & Associates

INTERNET
Go to any Internet search engine and look up the words *proposal, grants, foundations, contributions, giving, philanthropy, government funding, Federal Register, HUD*. There is a vast amount of information on the World Wide Web.

FOUR POINTS IN SETTING UP A COMPANY
1. **File Articles of Incorporation.**
   This is filed with the state Department of Assessments and Taxation. The Articles state the name of the corporation being formed and the purpose of the corporation. It provides information on the board of directors and who they are. The Articles are finalized, signed and dated by the president of the corporation.
2. **Draw up by-laws for the corporation.**
   This is the governing document for the corporation. It lists information such as where the officers are located, when meetings are being held, directors' and officers' names, interpretations and amendments (changes) to the by-laws. The by-laws are signed by the secretary of the corporation and are filed in the main operations office.

3. **File for tax-exempt status—501(c)3.**
   File an application for recognition of exemption on Form 1023, available from your local IRS office. The form will ask general and financial questions regarding the corporation filing for 501(c)3 status. An application fee, determined by Form 8718, applies.

4. **Letter of determination.**
   The Internal Revenue Service will mail a letter stating whether you have been given tax-exempt status under 501(c)3.

* NOTE: For further information on how to start a program for your own church or group, please contact Rock City Church.

The Story Of Columbine

Excerpt from *The Martyrs' Torch:*
The Message of the Columbine Story

"I am not going to apologize for speaking the name of Jesus,
I am not going to justify my faith to them,
and I am not going to hide the light that God has put into
me. If I have to sacrifice everything... I will. I will take it."

Personal Journal Entry, Rachel Joy Scott, April 20, 1998

The blood of the martyrs is the seed of the church.

Tertullian

After her death, Rachel's family discovered her personal journals. They revealed a deep, secret relationship with Jesus that even her family knew little about. Rachel walked in a depth of relationship with Jesus that displayed a wisdom far beyond her years, and she actually seemed to foreshadow her death in several entries.

One of her personal journals was delayed in being returned to her family for several weeks after her death because it was in her backpack when she died. One of the bullets that passed through her small body was discovered inside her backpack and was considered police evidence until officially released. This bloodstained journal portion is breathtaking in ways you will soon discover.

Rachel surely loved her mother and father very much. Tragically, her family was all too typical of so many broken homes in our times. In her younger years, her dad was a pastor and her family a typical pastor's family. Sadly, in spite of such a nurturing, spiritual family structure, her mother and father tragically divorced more than ten years ago, when Rachel was a young child. After the divorce was final, Beth and Darrell had joint custody of the five children, Bethanee, Dana, Rachel, Craig, and Mike.

During those years Beth scrimped and saved, going to school at night while working during the day to support her children. Her son Craig once told me that he would sometimes hear her praying and crying in her bedroom late at night when times were especially hard.

A few days before Mother's Day, just weeks after Rachel's death, Beth was tenderly going through some of her daughter's many writings and drawings. From one of the stacks of papers, a page fell out into Beth's hands. There, in the beautiful script that only Rachel could write, and as a timely gift from a most loving heavenly Father, was the following poem:

SACRIFICE
should be her name,
because she has given up so much for us.

HUMBLE
should be her name,
because she will never admit the great things she has done.

FAITH
should be her name,
because she has enough to carry us, as well as herself,
through this crazy world.

STRENGTH
should be her name,
because she had enough to bear and take care of five children.

WISDOM
should be her name,
because her words and knowledge are worth more than gold.

BEAUTIFUL
should be her name,
because it is not only evident in her face,
but in her heart and soul as well.

GRACEFUL
should be her name,
because she carries herself as true woman of God.

LOVING
should be her name,
because of the deepness of each hug and kiss she gives us.

ELIZABETH
is her name,
but I call her giving, humble, faithful,
strong, wise, beautiful, graceful, loving mom.

What mother does not yearn to hear such words of tender devotion from her daughter? Rachel has been described by her family as possessing a certain impish joy and uninhibited zeal for life. She would wear funny hats and took joy in wearing clothes that set the pace for fashion as she saw it. Her sisters told me that Rachel once put a message on the family phone recorder that said, "Hello, this is Princess Rachel. Which of her loyal subjects would you like to speak with?" Never at a loss for words, Rachel would say what she thought or felt, and she had a certain refreshing transparency toward everyone. She possessed a highly creative music talent. Her friends spoke of how she would sit at the piano and play the most beautiful music, enrapturing her listeners. When they begged her to play it again, she'd giggle and say she couldn't remember it because she had just made it up!

Once, while performing the mime presentation of "Watch the Lamb" to the music of Ray Boltz to her schoolmates at Columbine, the music suddenly stopped right in the middle of the performace. Well, Rachel just kept dancing! She went faithfully through the motions of her performance while several of her schoolmates chuckled. At last, when the music finally came on again, she was perfectly in sync with it! Everyone was amazed and moved by Rachel's tenacious determination. She won the respect of her classmates that night.

What was ironic about this incident is the fact that the young man who ran the sound system that evening was none other than Dylan Klebold. The music stopped in Rachel's life once, but she kept dancing. The second and final time the music stopped was when Rachel was killed. She is still dancing! No evil or power on earth can stop the heavenly music to which Rachel Joy Scott dances now.

Rachel's journals clearly reveal that she believed her time on earth would be brief. Her writings show a young woman fervent in her desire to serve God. Following is the last known entry in her dairy.

"Am I the only one who sees?
Am I the only one who craves Your glory?
Am I the only one who longs to be forever in Your loving arms?
All I want is for someone to walk with me through
these halls of a tragedy.
Please give me a loving friend who will carry Your name in the end.
Someone who longs to be with You.
Someone who will stay forever true."

At the Columbine Torchgrab Youth Rally, held in Littleton on August 7, Rachel's 16-year-old brother, Craig, said of his sister:...

The Martyrs' Torch
ISBN 0-7864-2046-6

Available at your local Christian bookstore.

For more information and sample chapters, visit www.reapernet.com

National Best-Selling Author
Tommy Tenney

THE GOD CHASERS

(Best-selling **Destiny Image** book)

There are those so hungry, so desperate for His presence, that they become consumed with finding Him. Their longing for Him moves them to do what they would otherwise never do: Chase God. But what does it really mean to chase God? Can He be "caught"? Is there an end to the thirsting of man's soul for Him? Meet Tommy Tenney—God chaser. Join him in his search for God. Follow him as he ignores the maze of religious tradition and finds himself, not chasing God, but to his utter amazement, caught by the One he had chased.

ISBN 0-7684-2016-4

GOD CHASERS DAILY MEDITATION & PERSONAL JOURNAL

Does your heart yearn to have an intimate relationship with your Lord? Perhaps you long to draw closer to your heavenly Father, but you don't know how or where to start. This *Daily Meditation & Personal Journal* will help you begin a journey that will change your life. As you read and journal, you'll find your spirit running to meet Him with a desire and fervor you've never before experienced. Let your heart hunger propel you into the chase of your life...after God!

ISBN 0-7684-2040-7

GOD'S FAVORITE HOUSE

The burning desire of your heart can be fulfilled. God is looking for people just like you. He is a Lover in search of a people who will love Him in return. He is far more interested in you than He is interested in a building. He would hush all of Heaven's hosts to listen to your voice raised in heartfelt love songs to Him. This book will show you how to build a house of worship within, fulfilling your heart's desire and His!

ISBN 0-7684-2043-1

Available at your local Christian bookstore.

For more information and sample chapters, visit www.reapernet.com

6B-1:2